THE CALGARY RENAISSANCE

THE CALGARY RENAISSANCE

*edited by
derek beaulieu &
rob mclennan*

CHAUDIERE BOOKS   MMXVI

TABLE OF CONTENTS

09   *derek beaulieu and rob mclennan*
Introduction

14   *Hollie Adams*
Project Description By: Jenny Weingarten

17   *Jonathan Ball*
As We All Should Lie

22   *Braydon Beaulieu*
In the Aurora

27   *Christian Bök*
from Colony Collapse Disorder

32   *Louis Cabri*
Flags of convenience

39   *Natalee Caple*
For Sandy Pool
Packing for the Weekend
For Nicole Markotić

42   *Weyman Chan*
Unboxing The Clone (excerpt from Human Tissue)

48   *Jason Christie*
This poem is a ski mask
Skeuomorph
I know how to deal with people like me

54   *Chris Ewart*
     The Chickpea Test

58   *Aaron Giovannone*
     from The Nonnets

60   *Helen Hajnoczky*
     Other Observations

65   *Susan Holbrook*
     What Is Poetry? (a twelve-tone poem)
     What is Prose?
     Without You

69   *Ken Hunt*
     Probes
     Phage
     In the Shadow of the Moon

74   *Jani Krulc*
     The Unicorn Parade

83   *Larissa Lai*
     goodbye butterfly, hello kitty: an opiate opera

98   *Naomi K. Lewis*
     Eye

103 *Nicole Markotić*
     hand-in-hand

109	*Suzette Mayr*	
	Crawley Hall	
110	*kevin mcpherson eckhoff*	
	Unhold Fiends	
114	*Sandy Pool*	
	On Anatomical Procedures	
115	*Sharanpal Ruprai*	
	One Strand at a Time	
117	*Ian Sampson*	
	The Tale of Pinuccio and Niccolosa	
124	*Jordan Scott*	
	Dawn from *The Day Book*	
131	*Nikki Sheppy*	
	HEX^{bugonia}	
	aestheticize	
134	*Natalie Simpson*	
	Rapt fractures I-IV	
136	*Emily Ursuliak*	
	Removing the Shoe	
142	*Natalie Zina Walschots*	
	Stephanie McMahon's Perfect Eyeliner	
	Heavy Metals	

145 *Andrew Wedderburn*
Everything Else is Scale
Up-Belt

148 *Julia Williams*
from Share React: A Memoir in Four Children's Books

151 *Rita Wong*
sunset grocery
grammar poem

155 *Eric Zboya*
Gallus
Solarium 1

157 *Paul Zits*
The destructive impulse becomes automatic
The stirring of the slated metal blinds

163 Contributors

THE SHAPE OF CITIES: THE CALGARY RENAISSANCE
rob mclennan

Long before I spent my nine months in Edmonton as writer-in-residence at the University of Alberta, I'd been curious as to how the writing of the two major cities in Alberta had been shaped into what they had become, but it was only during that period, the 2007-8 academic year, that I was able to really consider each city up close. Edmonton was home to two major literary presses and almost no little magazine and/or reading series culture, and Calgary managed to be its complete opposite, even as both have enjoyed waves of literary activities orbiting their universities and beyond. How do cities themselves get made, and the writing therein? The community of writers that have centred around, through and beyond such past and present Calgary-based journals and presses as *filling Station*, No Press, MODL Press, *dANDelion*, housepress, *secrets from the orange couch, endnote, NōD magazine* and *(orange)*, are remarkably deliberate and vibrant, despite whatever breaks and disturbances and hardships any normal community are bound to endure.

It was also during my time in Alberta that the idea for an anthology of Calgary writing first took hold. In Hiromi Goto's biographical note at the back of the fiction anthology *And Other Stories* (Talonbooks, 2001), editor George Bowering added that she was "part of the Calgary renaissance." It was an innocent enough throw-away, something that many readers of the collection probably didn't catch, but it was astute editor Bowering pointing out that something had been happening out there that required acknowledgment. Calgary's literary engagement was also strengthened by the presence of writer-mentors Aritha van Herk and Fred Wah, allowing the city to further develop a uniquely strong, supportive and varied community of writers working with more radical forms.

Over the past two decades-plus, there has been a definite shift in "prairie poetics," moving through and out the other side of the geographies of, say, poets such as Andrew Suknaski, Lorna Crozier, Dennis Cooley, Eli Mandel, Kristjana Gunnars and Robert Kroetsch into further, more radicalized forms, as in the works of a number of former and current Calgary writers we fortunate were able to include in the current volume. For the past decade or two, many of the writers collected here have been moving away from more traditional forms into more "radical" territory through lyric fiction, concrete/visual poetry, conceptual works, post-lyric, homolinguistic translation and other forms. Engaged in an aesthetics of change, Calgary has become an essential centre for such changes that derek beaulieu once described, in an essay on Calgary poetics in *Open Letter,* as "left-wing social politics, radical linguistic structures and an inner-city urban environment as compositional and theoretical frameworks for poetic discourse."

RESIDENTS AND TOURISTS: THE CALGARY RENAISSANCE
Derek Beaulieu

As Calgary's 2014–2016 Poet Laureate, it was my distinct pleasure to be an artistic ambassador for the city, presenting at events and producing literary work that reflected our city and its citizens both locally and internationally. When I was interviewed for the position I entered the discussion with one task in mind: to honour and recognize the city's rich literary history: journalists, novelists, poets, playwrights. The role of the Poet Laureate is to be reflective of, and responsive to, community. To dialogue, teach, learn and listen—to provoke, initiate, inspire ... and *to remember*.

The citizens of Calgary tend to be unaware of our rich literary community; of the writers who have walked our pathways and lived in our neighbourhoods. With their passing, they fall out of our collective imaginations and back on to our shelves. Their books become silent footnotes to the communities that they helped build, reflect, document and enrich. A city's literature makes tangible our citizen's thoughts and concerns, our triumphs and our shame, our small personal reflections and our larger civic discourses. I learn of Calgary and its growth through its literature, through its authors and poets.

Robert Kroetsch lived in Calgary for only a few years, but as the author of 9 novels, 13 collections of poetry and 17 other collections, his writing represented the myths and stories of Albertan culture that continue to enthuse. Among his many titles Kroetsch's influential book of poetry *Seed Catalogue* (1977) was inspired by his finding an old seed catalogue at the Glenbow Museum. Kroetsch described Calgarian printmaker John Snow's house as "a house full of art. Crammed full of travel and creation"—an easy way of understanding Calgary itself.

It is all too easy to forget our authors and how they articulate our space. The city of Calgary has not celebrated our artistic history on our streets—unlike many other cities we do not have monuments, plaques, street-signs, parks or public spaces named after our authors—but they are there. Our writers craft our imaginations, they testify to the importance of community and the vitality of the arts. They write our city.

A friend of mine recently categorized New York City's population in to two groups: residents and tourists; neither of which are based on where people are from. Tourists arrive in the city to absorb, to learn from, to "take" something and then return home. Residents, as part of living in the city, give back to the city, they learn with and teach; they make the city what it is.

Over the last several decades, Calgary's literary community has been exemplified by a community of residents—of authors, poets, community organizers, hosts, editors, teachers, professors and funders—who have dedicated their practice to giving back to the conversation. Calgary's community has, for decades, been focussed on the exploration of the edges of language, the experimental potential of poetry and prose.

The Calgary Renaissance explores a selection of several generations of authors who have centred around grass-roots, community-driven venues for literary exploration: *NōD* magazine, *dANDelion magazine* and *filling Station magazine* (and its reading series, *flywheel,* and rambunctious literary festival *Blow-out*), the small press community and the on-going mentorship and instruction at the Mount Royal University, the University of Calgary and the Alberta College of Art + Design. It is a love letter to several generations of Calgarian authors who have decided to give back, and become part of a conversation around what language can do—they have created a city internationally renowned for its vibrant, challenging literary community.

PROJECT DESCRIPTION BY: JENNY WEINGARTEN
Hollie Adams

My proposed final project for your Fall 2013 Creative Writing IV workshop class is a short story which will take the form of a proposal, not unlike the form of this very proposal, in which the student-narrator proposes to compose a short story in the form of a proposal. Should I be accepted into your class this coming semester, my proposed final project will mimic the rhetoric of a formal proposal of an academic project (or in this case, creative project, though I think you will see that it has a strong theoretical framework as well, as it grapples with the narratological concepts of narrator vs. narratee and implied author vs. implied reader, as well as issues of narrative voice and focalization, ideas you so helpfully illuminated in this past semester's workshop class [i.e., Creative Writing III] in which I was enrolled and in which, as you know, I received a grade of A which I believe I was awarded for the merit of my writing alone and not certain external factors of no real relevance to the course and which rightly had no bearing, positive or otherwise, on my performance therein, and therefore it goes without saying that such factors will not influence the decision [re: my admittance] of someone as professional as yourself, even though certain statements have been made which could be interpreted to insinuate the contrary).

Yet, through this playful imitation of the academic/creative proposal, a cogent narrative will begin to take shape indirectly rather than directly. It is my intention that the reader will begin to glean insights into the character of the protagonist (i.e., the student-narrator) via the language she employs (i.e., her intelligence, ambition, and guarded professionalism), as well as insights into the nature of the relationship of the student and the professor via the manner in which the former addresses the latter (i.e., their level of "familiarity" [clearly she has studied under this professor before], or perhaps more succinctly put, "intimacy" [she will mention in her proposal "certain external factors" which the reader will rightly suspect involve the professor in some way]).

I feel the need to emphatically state here that my short story in the form of a proposal will, of course, be fictional—and I am sure it goes without saying that I intend for the reader (namely, my future classmates and, more importantly, yourself) to differentiate between the character of the author (i.e., me) and the character of my protagonist (i.e., the female student-narrator). As you continually reminded us last semester in Creative Writing III, we (i.e., the inexperienced, naive undergraduates) should never confuse the author with the narrator even when the distance between the two seems minimal, even when we believe the work to be vaguely—or even chiefly—autobiographical.

The short story that the student-narrator proposes, however, is meant to be read as only a slightly-fictionalized, or perhaps non-fictionalized (though I intend to leave this ambiguous), account of her affair with her much older, married Creative Writing professor, in whose class she was enrolled the previous semester (let's call it "Creative Writing III"). While yes, even as an "inexperienced," "naive" undergraduate, I realize that we (i.e., not you because you are clearly experienced and, what is the best word for "not naive"? Perhaps "jaded asshole"?) should never confuse the author and the narrator, I also realize that readers do often confuse the two. All a writer needs to do is give his/her character his/her own name and voila! Confusion. It is this confusion I intend to make use of in the short story I propose to compose in the form of a proposal. Even though the student-narrator will emphatically claim her short story is a purely fictional one, much as I have above, I intend for the reader to conflate the student-narrator (i.e., the implied author of the proposal/short story) and her proposed protagonist (i.e., her own student-narrator). Let's call my student-narrator "Jenny" and let's say she calls her own proposed narrator "Jenny" even as she (i.e., Jenny the first) insists she is writing (or proposing to write) a fictional story and it is only coincidental that her protagonist-narrator (i.e., Jenny the second) should have the same name as she does (i.e., the same name as my proposed student-narrator). Too much confusion? Perhaps there will be no names at all.

Still, as the student-narrator's proposal, and thus short story, continues, it becomes clear that the professor with whom she has had the affair and the professor to whose class she hopes to gain admittance (let's call it "Creative Writing IV") via her proposal are one and the same (i.e., her narratee and also her implied reader, in this case, are the professor who also serves as the antagonist [i.e., "jaded asshole"] in the narrative that is swiftly developing as the proposal continues). It also becomes clear that this same Creative Writing professor would like to prevent this student-narrator from enrolling in his upcoming class ("Creative Writing IV")—she will, for instance, make use of the passive voice in sentences like "certain statements have been made"—due to their past relationship ("external factors"), which he, citing moral objection and marital obligation, has swiftly ended (though he had never once previously spoken to the student-narrator regarding any such morals and often referred, pre-coitus, to the marriage in question as "already over").

Should I be accepted into Creative Writing IV, I have no doubt that with your guidance and constructive criticism, as well as the feedback I receive from the rest of the class, my proposed short story, the tentatively-titled "Project Description," can become successful as both an experiment in narration and a psychological study of two—again, I emphasize—fictional characters.

Please find my writing sample attached.

AS WE ALL SHOULD LIE
Jonathan Ball

Whatever happened took place in the night. When I awoke, when we all awoke, our backyards, once separated by thin fences, stood a full block apart. Divided by a large, empty lot and two thin streets.

I first saw this new block that had sprung from the ether when I went out to feed Einstein, stupidest of dogs. The invisible hands that reshaped the land had met in my backyard just inside the fence. When they pulled apart to separate my once-neighbour Sarah from me, they dragged the once-common fence along with her. And from my now-fenceless backyard the dog had fled. As though from so tremendous a force there could be some banal escape.

I stepped out into the impossible street that ran where Sarah's yard had once lain. It supported me like a real street would. Already there were potholes. A car's horn jarred me back into the house.

In the kitchen I stared into an empty cup. Then the doorbell rang. Sarah. From across the new block. She told me she'd driven around it rather than walk across.

Then madness, a flood of people, conferences on back lawns, across remaining fences — talk, endless talk, and at the end of the day, at the end of it all, we still knew nothing, know nothing.

ᴓ

City officials grumbled about whose problem this was, this impossible block. While they argued, they sent forth surveyors. Then fired them and sent forth more. When the second team came back with the same findings for which the first was fired, a chill settled into the city that even the record summer heat could not drive out.

The surveyors agreed that although this new block *did* take up space, it nevertheless *did not* alter the physical landscape outside of its immediate area. The block appeared between 3rd St. and 4th St., below 16th Ave. and above 15th Ave., but these streets stood unmoved. Nothing had been changed in the surrounding landscape, but somehow the block had been added — the empty block and its new framing streets, which connected to the aforementioned avenues as if having been there always.

And yet the block did not change the world around it. The streets remained straight, did not bulge.

There was just *more* in the city now, *more* between those streets than before. There was *more* and the *more* could be measured. Static and unchanging. Abiding by the physical laws of this universe, although its appearance and persistence stood in plain refutation of those laws.

A bubble — a rectangular, block-shaped bubble — had erupted in the fabric of space and *more* of the world had risen to fill it, without otherwise disturbing the surface of the (until now) ordinary world.

※

Dazed and panicked, City Hall responded with insane disavowal in true bureaucratic form. It named the new streets 3A and 4A and announced that, pending negative results of a test for radiation at the site, its real estate would be zoned residentially (in accordance with the surrounding area) and auctioned off.

Almost immediately, a fierce bidding war ensued, driving the property value of the now-named "Block A" up beyond meaning. While developers fought, and Calgary rushed to introduce a complex array of senseless bylaws, in a strange turn the property value of everything surrounding Block A plummeted. Nobody wanted to live near this philosophical disaster.

Everyone else sold, most to speculators who intended to hold the property while staying far away from their new "homes." Only I remained after the first night. The others in the neighbourhood stayed with friends, family, lovers, or in hotels until their sales went through. Sarah moved back in with her ex-husband.

I stayed in case Einstein returned. And every morning stepped out back into the nightmare. Before she left, Sarah begged me to come with her. She knew that I had no one, said that David wouldn't mind. Of course he would have, but it didn't matter. I had to stay.

֍

Soon, crowds appeared. Tourists, first from across the city, but then from across the globe. As Block A became international news, a steady stream of travellers arrived, suitcases bursting with excitement. First, they circled the block. Then, after they'd built up enough courage, stepped into the heart of its mystery. Then nothing. Despite its extraordinary origins, Block A disappointed. A browning field of grass between two thin strips of pockmarked pavement.

The crowds dwindled, but interest in the block renewed when a mad development firm succeeded in securing the land rights. They brought in an avant-garde architect to design the new houses, which spilled over and twisted around one another, often sharing walls, almost sharing rooms, in some snaking perversion of suburbia that might have seemed natural in a parallel universe. Although these houses depressed the property values of the surrounding homes even further, they themselves demanded incredible prices.

For a while, then, Block A became home to wealthy eccentrics who were happy enough living there, although discouraged each morning to find they had not been whisked away by aliens or into an inter-dimensional portal during the night. And on the edge of this horror, amidst decaying homes, my modest bungalow. This senseless vigil.

⁂

Sarah started calling. She never visited. She began reminiscing about the years we'd known each other, as if talking to a friend at my funeral. Then she started confessing secrets to me, as if I were a nameless listener on a help line. Then she called to say I scared her and she never called again.

⁂

People speculated on the cause of the block's appearance, the most popular conspiracy theories involving extraterrestrials or terrorists. A gaggle of scientists secured research grants to study the area, but learned nothing. Block A became a hot academic topic, but hundreds of doctoral theses and journal articles later, the world was no closer to any sensible answer to its quiet but unceasing question.

It became apparent that Block A intended to neither yield its mysteries nor produce new ones. Fascination dimmed and then diminished. The eccentrics moved away and let their twisted mansions rot.

Though Block A left an indelible mark upon the planet's skin, it did nothing to aggravate the wound. The world went on, dragging Block A with it. Assimilated into a universe that refused its possibility but had not denied its entry.

As for me, I wrote this down. But it was difficult and took many years. And yet so much is missing. The account so short, unremarkable — unrevealing.

How is it that impossible things can appear, spit blank stares into our faces, and remain mute? Since we cannot look away, after some initial panic we make a show of ignoring them.

But I refuse to ignore this. I no longer sleep at night, surrounded by empty houses, with this chaos out the window at the foot of my bed. I no longer sleep, I just pretend.

I lie awake, as we all should lie, and await the coming of Block B.

IN THE AURORA
Braydon Beaulieu

i.

The bricks inhale a boomerang. I name the writer. I splutter ivory gutters up the alley. I name the artist: cherry drizzle arching through the coulisse. My whirlbat ricochets off concrete and spills, crimson, over shoulders. These bracers, knives in a firing line from the forge. Is it fierce to bare in the face of asylum? Is it a skyline through autumn fog? These pages that flutter in the breezeway, that echo in the street, that alight on cars and fold their red wings.

ii.

For safe walks home from the pub. For acid not bombing in the smog. For justice, as he might say. What might he say? I knew he might turn up on some rooftop somewhere. Star power in the post-Halloween world. He wears the river around his neck, and its rapids roil down his back. I correct his math. Repel his ink. I'll wear my hair however I want to, thank you very much. Petrichor rises and dampens my cheeks. Lipstick enumerating the fluorescent lights that knead the thrum of city streets. The taillights that cut the shimmering asphalt. Candy smears and glints in the narrows.

iv.

This. This is my scar. Pigeons flutter just outside the glass. Slobber drips phosphorescent from the mouths of the coven. And this. This is my body. These, my wings. Red standards rippling just outside the floodlight. An extinguished E that used to run royal. The dust of old books. A lilt in the flagpole and a skull without a jawbone. Light weeps through the stained glass and crumples against the cobblestone. Names have power. I name myself. I'm not your crescent character. I wax. I wane. I breathe full and new in the aurora.

vi.

My wings unfurl in the dusk. I curl through the haze in a parabolic arc above a fragmenting bullet, an amber starburst. My bleeds drain blind in the gutters at the edge of cardamom. But still, my father clings to burlap sacks. Dabs his palate with peppercorn. He's umber. He's ash. Does ink really brush ink? Do fossils float at the edge of the atmosphere? If I breathe, will my lungs collapse? His grief swells to the point of rain. My armour rusts into autumn. Leaves blow in from the Palisades to lament under shoes. Swans head south from the river, and pigeons huddle close on the sidewalks. These. These are my arches, my leaves, my pearls. Aluminum laces my tongue and my throat. Rime ascends the edge of a dagger. Every surface in the sky gets a new skin. And this. This is my face. This, my crown. An obelisk in the city centre. Map it. Reach out and touch it. Come home.

vii.

I name the protagonist: me. The sheen traces my new skin. Bulrushes whip in the gale. The green aurora beacons over the harbours. I'm not your poem. I'm not your muse. I live up here, in this sky. And you, you seek the water. Stop. It's over. This. Your body. These. Your eyes. We fly, suspended over the river. Palms brushing palms. I hold on tight as I can. Linger over shades of blue. Every stroke of cerulean. Azure. Indigo and iris. Trickles of pearl and drops of peach. Goldenrod reflected by the shoreline. The copper edge of the coast. And let go.

FROM COLONY COLLAPSE DISORDER
Christian Bök

Exordium

European honeybees (*Apis mellifera*) have suffered from a pandemic syndrome that causes workers to forsake their duties, foraging without returning home, leaving the queen and her brood unattended, until the hive itself dwindles into abandonment; moreover, any stores of honey in the forsaken dwelling often go unlooted by other pests for much longer than expected. While entomologists have proposed several factors that might account for this disorder (including bouts of infection by either varroa mites or fungal smuts), the problem is likely aggravated by the broad usage of the pesticide, imidacloprid, a neonicotinoid that can disrupt the nervous systems of bees, impairing their ability to navigate. The disorder threatens this species of insect with extinction — thus posing a danger to the welfare of humanity, which relies upon such bees to pollinate crops.

Chensheng Lu, et al. 'Sublethal Exposure to Neonicotinoids Impaired Honey Bees' Winterization Before Proceeding to Colony Collapse Disorder.' *Bulletin of Insectology* 67.1 (2014): 125-130.

1. *(On the Apiary of the World)*

Airborne honeydew sweetens my spirit
with a perfume that, by divine decree,
hath enticed me to perform these sonnets
for thee, my mæstro, Gaius Mæcenas.
Study, with grimness, the plight of puny
gods – warlords in a daylong dynasty,
whose sieges and jihads I must belaud
in song. Scant be my labour, but not my
reward, if Apollo favours these rhymes.
Annex first to the hive, a haven, blind
to winds that hinder foragers in flight,
then suffer neither yak nor ewe to trek
across these meadows, nor oxen to dash
away the dew from phloxes and grasses.

2.

Disperse from thy honied stalls the gaily
tinted geckos, then repel the red-plumed
bee-eaters, which echo flocks of swallows
(the progeny of Procne, her blouse still
bloody from her filicide). Let no throng
of songbirds indulge in such butchery,
by which a bee, tweezed in a beak, is fed
to savage broods, like a dainty morsel,
but let some streamlet of meltwater run
near mossy pools of greenery, then let
the fronds of betel palms or olive trees
drape each entryway to thy catacomb,
wherefrom the oligarchs at dawn deploy
their convoy of drones on vernal forays.

3.

Thistles and brambles by the riverside
beckon thy scouts from the toil of travel
to rest awhile in hidden groves of shade.
Upon the shallows, whether swift or still,
place a willow bough or a paving stone
– a footbridge for the flyers that alight
to preen each winglet made of diaphane
(for Eurus often bids the sudden breeze
to douse such envoys in spritzes of mist
or drown such pilots in speckles of rain).
Let flower beds of basil, thyme, and clove
overgrow these clover fields, the fiefdoms
of the hive, heavy-laden with the musk
of violets, overwhelming thy wellsprings.

4.

Contrive that the ingress to the sanctum
of the bees be narrow, made from woven
osiers or cedar braids, for summer heat
can soften firm taffies and winter cold
can curdle warm jellies, both disastrous
for these denizens, who must fix a hole
in each wall of wax, filling this fissure
with their pollen, then sealing the crevice
with their saliva, a spittle, which binds
more fast than any glue, be it coal tar
or pine gum, from the hills of Phrygia.
True to fame, all bees at home in foxholes
can nest in the clefts of each hollow karst,
if not in the chinks of some fallen birch.

FLAGS OF CONVENIENCE
Louis Cabri

The argument

Kool & the Gang, "Celebration"; Detroit River, Nov 2014, "Live Ships Map – Vessel Traffic and Positions" MarineTraffic.com; Peter Goodspeed, "Can Canada duplicate its boat people rescue with Syrian refugees?" TheStar.com Fri Sep 26 2014; Darlene Keju, "Speech to the World Council of Churches Assembly, Vancouver, 1983" Youtube

Kaye E. Barker

OK, you are now chairwoman of the Marystown Chapter

Come on!

abandoned his book on 'Haykel' and founded Operation Lifeline

Ce-le-brex time

(Zo-loft!)

Federal Kumano

Zoloft Apartments

Asteline Reunion Hall

Asteline!

Oh Asteline

leeward Howard Adelman

Algosoo

Treximet
Prozatene idle

Nexium
Catullus

Catullus

Sarah Desgagnés

Levitrain chaintion Vioxx way

Federal Kumano

Nexium comparator
Pristiq

Pristiq bounty

Kimono Condoms

Lavoris orange (sponge)

Vytorin head plate

Rebecca Lynn plate

Retaphin dolphination

Orsula

via cargo

ship interview

ing people

fallout

Abilify
jest

club Abilify
jelly Vioxx sway

calendrical

Darlene Keju

Humira ship
ping container Zoloft apartments

Crestor, tanker

Focalin

Ken Boothe Sr

He's also moved to the absolute top of his class in all subjects (excerpt for his writing lol)

Vyvanse

Vyvanse!

Federal Kumano

Cymbalta union

Niaspan incursive

Dick Beddoes

Kimono

Condo minimums

hull strength at full draught

Advair

Nair

pristine

ninnity

in *add*

year none

of us spoke

English pass

partout

Viet name ease, Syrian plea

Come on

FOR SANDY POOL
Natalee Caple

say nothing against darkening
no small argument with wings
sings hands rubbing eyelashes

opalled eyes reflect the wet
throat made sweet with honeycomb
say nothing against darkening

all morning long the clapboard fence
is polished by the sun
sings hands rubbing eyelashes

say nothing against darkening
so lovely are your shoulders
somewhere someone licks your heart

waits to say how
he and she or she and she or they and they
become luminous companions
say nothing against darkening

PACKING FOR THE WEEKEND (FOR NATALIE WALSCHOTS)
Natalee Caple

my boxing gloves
my gumballs
my dental floss
my computer
my concave mask
my jetpack
my thrusters on high
my fickle wits
my trigger finger
my razor wire
my cocksure pink connections
my electrochemical insulation
my lethal hummingbird
my broomstick bombs
my matches
my green sticky bone saw
my warbled earthquake kiss
my piano-limbed internet trolls
my tarred generation
my beloveds

FOR NICOLE MARKOTIC
Natalee Caple

In August it rains and rains

I slosh more wine into my brains

until I breathe wine

You lick the back of my knees

I touch your fingers

propose we build a bridge

be minotaurs in alphabets

sew triangles over scars

knit hymens for all kinds of birds

I will write you a slim letter

Someday

UNBOXING THE CLONE
(EXCERPT FROM HUMAN TISSUE)
Weyman Chan

    11.1

Embedded in human tissue are anachronistic codas, from an age of hopeless idealism

lips don't stray from their prayerbook

nor do introns, sleepy gestures and non-expressed junk-garble, a sizeable, excisable foreskin that for some reason gets a free pass into the next generation's genome—

                                  waekup Waeymn, wh

        ere am I

           hven't bin myself in a longtime
indelible wink on numbers and laws, dial tones and shipwrecks, can spoof a myriad of ex vivo transferases wet-laced by said apoptotic vector

already you are the future, as all futures build

                            self from a child's underpulse.

Violence girds innocence, raised as its own subject.

What now? Chastened and atomized by useless possibility, say, of a failed Ming coordinate system, Flash Gordon's graphite tights would makes petri dishes of us all. You can pocket all the alanines and thymines you want. Signature linkages of life mean to drive patent anastomoses pingponged from Brownian primordiality, unzipped mouths of filmy substrate, embryonic Last Girls heated and cooled on brackish shores.

Time will annihilate you, says the master of screwed-in prosthetics. It will compose

your failure, as you consume, adapt, conflate.

11.84

Social environment—what a concept—

Babs again. Her social worker's voice.

Codespread = wordkey. Acid deniability distances the prototype. Do not share codespread with any other. You shall have no codespread but your own.

0.0089

eukaryotic mush phagocytized the void

(expansion constant) – (funeral white) = N

historic truth must nonetheless ink the mind while our open-sourced disassembly

(my Chineseness)

like poignant exhaust touching itself

amends Rorschachs that stick Cruella on the same easy listening chart as Mao, baubles bromating banter from thought-wielding phonemes hived in every cell

to beguile fortune

                you wrestle doubt

(swamp hordes of the Tethys sea threading telomere to photon receptor)

                because

      raising any other

      slug

      is to foil the singularity

2

what would our futures see

if sharing had no clearer void than to be left alone to ponder,
every Queer Dog Convention richer than castrati

                                            in kinshyp ther

post-connective breach subsidizes Snowden's Chinese comedy

                          word-rap over tissue wreck, you say

cognition's encipherment spreads its nowhere-pillow

                              curled up in drawn out fury

first-to-third base desperation, overstated and quickly banished to
the exigency of tight-ass dots that cross your preludes

                            what would your future see

if you were told you were in a black box, and the creator
wouldn't open it because she wanted you to be both alive and
dead? Is meta-resignation enough to satisfy bad potential?

                            I think

                            therefore I don't exist unless I speak

is our counter-bait, our censure, our web circuitry

2.3

long ago, human tissue grew Newtonian sails to distance allegory from its material directrix

        under guise of woodland

        breezes pollinating lithesome bowers

rods and cones plexiformed behind a protein window

tissue breathed, so CO^2 buildup wouldn't bind angiotensins or let calcium channels seize

some other delicious algebra to expunge those bleak batons on Pussy Riot

recursive bruise envy

at the immortal hem of the weaver and the cowherd

    separated by their milky way   only once a year are they

joined

for whom the seduction, a bridge built by magpies, binds dew to a corolla's throated proscenium

biota on the head of a pin

more love to lose, by which the world punishes

but wait   I'

m from the future, listen up   I

bring you alchemy in a pill

THIS POEM IS A SKI MASK
Jason Christie

a target with no lines
no colour wheel or

a spin cycle class
on laundering intent

no fixed placard or
precarious labour or

around which to
announce an end

of us versus them
except who among us

and what of them
walks along the

olive branch
stretched across

whichever fake
divide suits

our causes?

what poem isn't a
valet for rich readers?

bottle service
stolen land

a vip seat
would you

sign the petition
for poets

against privilege?
it's on the other

side of this velvet rope

this poems is a ski mask
this poem hides in the garage
this poem features three knives
this poem waits for you
this poem wants for nothing
this isn't really a poem

some crushed diamonds
mixed with a residency
at a chalet in France
and never a whiff
of poetry as an object

in the strictest
technical sense

of an orange vapour
an unknown agent

a spectacular sunrise
or royalty cheque

the separate address
for this sole

proprietorship
in name only

sitting upright
citizens in name only

hunkering private-like
as the giant eye

swivels past
without pause

over where we live
us poets
in the know
in name only

SKEUOMORPH
Jason Christie

a little finger fading away
at dawn into the language
of sentiment and nostalgia

using a mouse not tapping
don't touch that
dial on your screen

stay tuned poetry
makes nothing into

something happening
turns dust into a sun-
dappled screen, or

images we never needed
a spoke, a paddle, a sail
images we never wanted
a fire, some smoke, a wave
fall away into metaphor

remember the woods
paneling the countryside
or the granite spray
with which to lacquer
every available surface?

what i wanted to say

recedes into a poem
the many-nettled beam
or the encrusted oak
now fallen into disuse
a Faberge omelet with Chablis
at a dinner table for nobody

I KNOW HOW TO DEAL WITH PEOPLE LIKE ME
Jason Christie

a little ice patch
between friends
dropped in place

permafrost pitch
a pond upon which
everything thins

thinking lange
but meaning
ursprach as long
as it continues to exist

the ice upon which
i will eventually slip

a moment in transit
a note from one trick
on a box and
the next second
an exemplary code
of conduct
labeled: only
for public use

THE CHICKPEA TEST
Chris Ewart

Gabby's Man fits a fine khaki suit and twenty-four-karat-gold cufflinks just right. The gold is real in 1972 and so is marriage before having a child. When Gabby's Man gave Gabby a gold-and-diamond ring he told her, "Here, you can ski in the morning and swim in the sea in the afternoon." The ring fits on her finger oh so perfectly. Sparkily so. Gabby's Slim Groom has a sturdy gold tooth and a Mother, too.

Sturdy as a broom.

An activity for all seasons.

Gabby wears a dress of many flowers. Pink, yellow, tangerine, and bright blue – not quite the colour of forget-me-nots. Arm in arm on their way to his Mother's, a lady offers five American dollars for that dress of many flowers. Gabby loosens her grip on his hand.

It is hot in 1972, in June.

Shrugging florid shoulders she turns to The Lady. While a puff of ruby dust settles atop Gabby's thonged toes, she decides to sell the dress of many flowers.

Just like that.

Gabby's Slim Groom in the fine khaki suit parks his fine, slim shoes upon that same ruby dust. Sensing a pronounced nick his left twenty-four-karat-gold cufflink, he attempts willing it smooth. "Ouch!" Gabby strains, "Toes!" She pries those toes free and scuffs towards The Lady to sell that fancy-dancy dress for five American dollars. In the middle of the hot, hot day, on the side of the busy, nearly gritty street, she asks to be unzipped. Cars honk and whistles fly like butterflies towards Gabby's sun-ripened back.

A real pistachio cookie.

Her slip shines in the sun above the scarlet dust.

"Try this," The Lady insists, "to soothe your eyes and hair. They are like fire." The Lady smiles and pulls a soft cotton dress of lemon-yellow over Gabby's sweaty head, smoothing the fabric over her hips nearly to her knees – just covering that beacon of a slip.

Gabby loathes slips.

They remind her of medication.

"We're visiting his Mother. We're getting married." Gabby grins, baring most of her teeth and beaming in her new dress. With most of her fingers stretched out to cuticles she notices her diamond is real too. She's ready to conduct a twirl.

"Best of luck on the test," The Lady with the Dresses mentions, "Just keep smiling."

"Okay, um," Gabby clutches her five American dollars and skips back to her dustless groom, "thanks?" He likes her dress almost as much as his cufflinks and nods his approval.

Five American dollars is a lot of money in 1972.

She twirls once in that saffron-yellow dress as they almost dance a valeta up the hill to his Mother's sturdy house. "Waltzing dirties my shoes," claims Gabby's Slim Groom.

Zestfully so.

But before entering his Mother's house, Gabby has to wait outside its big red door.

Alone.

Not soon enough, Gabby's Slim Groom's Mother arrives at the door with a giant bowl of green and white gumballs. She glares at Gabby and says, "Take."

Almost a wince.

Gabby freezes in 1972, in June. Her hand refuses to move and her jaw starts to ache.

"Take one. You must!" His Mother winces indeed.

Gabby closes her eyes tight, her fingers stabbing deep, deep down into the belly of the bowl.

An icy pick.

She opens her eyes.

A poison pufferfish.

With great delight, Gabby's Slim Groom motions for her to chew, chew and chew. Like a hungry mime.

"I can't eat gum," she whispers oh so quietly. "It hurts my teeth."

Shatteringly so.

"Ah! Bad teeth!" his Mother yells. "I forbid you to marry my son!" The big red door of his Mother's sturdy house slams shut – cooling the beads of sweat on Gabby's forehead to tacks. Just like that.

The big red door was good and locked with Gabby's Slim Groom and his Mother inside. Not soon enough, Gabby swishes back down the hill. She weeps a little amongst the street's brown ochre dust. Just a little. She stops to smell some orange blossoms and tries her hand at weaving a few. "Gently tiring," she thinks, placing a loose band of them around her wrist, smudging pollen as she twists stems snug. "Instant breakfast," she sniffs. Though visions of Tang make her smile on the inside on such a hot, hot afternoon, she wears a frown until she happens upon The Lady with the Dresses and the five American dollars.

Instant breakfasts are popular in 1972.

"Failed the test, my girl? You must have bad teeth." The Lady with the dresses bares her roomy teeth with pride. "Why do you think I'm not married? There's no ring on my finger. Chickpeas are too hard for me!"

"Chickpeas?" Gabby wipes her pollen nose on her mustard-yellow dress. "They're not chickpeas, they're gum. Gum. Green and white gumballs. I can't eat gum. It aches too much."

The Lady with the Dresses wheezes, "Gum? Ha! Chickpeas, girl. Covered in sugar for surprise. If fancy-cuffs' Mother catches you reaching for your teeth then the wedding is finished! No bad teeth in the family." She pointed right into her mouth. "These two here. Finished weddings. And this one in the back? – finished!"

Gabby rubs her jaw with her left hand, impressed with The Lady with the Dresses' ability to speak clearly with a finger in her mouth. Gabby is not so chatty, but the sweet Tang of her new necklace does tickle her nose.

The Lady with the Dresses smiles again, fingers free of teeth, "You still have the ring, I see."

Gabby notices its sparkle. Just a little. Smoothing out the bumps of her new sunshine-yellow dress, she slows at her belly. Just so. "Thanks for the dress." Five American dollars is a lot of money in 1972.

FROM THE NONNETS
Aaron Giovannone

ITALICS LUXURIATE. THE letters recline, *literally*.
I am squishy on the inside
an unstable admixture, no simple mixture.

I squeeze an unripe avocado, calculating.
I have crunched the numbers
and I have crunched the celery stalks.

Soon I'll be old enough to believe
the music at Safeway is okay.
Even if I am wise, I will be wrong.

FROM THE NONNETS
Aaron Giovannone

THE NEIGHBOURHOOD SMELLS of lilacs
but how could I be so naive?
When they announced the evacuation on CBC

I stuffed the cupboards with books
piled them on the fridge.
Reader, I own very little.

Would you take me with you in a flood?
When I'm gone, you'll read this differently.
Am I gone yet?

OTHER OBSERVATIONS
Helen Hajnoczky

A flimsy crutch to hold the light,
Day's back strained against the night
We stroll in sunset's consumptive rattle;
He scuttles me through muffled streets,
Our tedious retreats
Drain hours like the sour aftertaste of milky tea
His company, the dregs of winter between my teeth:
Until some baleful fit guides his stupor
To lift a stammering hand to my back
And shuffle closer through the sawdust and ash …
To trawl me through still more stale roads
And cocoon me in dusk's colic glow

All too soon his fumbling gaze
Tugs the hemline of my ease.

The humid morning pressed against the evening rain,
Night's fresh breath crushed against the morning's rays,
Thick air wheezed upon the doors of the balcony,
Squeezed under the door cracks into the foyer,
Let the dawn cough its heat onto the still damp streets,
Breathe its stale breath, in sickly heaves,
Until the sharp teeth of evening rain,
Bite back the day's hacking heat.

And again and once again
The dawn will press its breath into the coiled streets,
Will crush its heat against the evening's sleet;

And then again and once again
I will wipe the makeup from my dripping face;
I will pull on and then pull off my lace,
Come home from work and pull off my heels
And sink into the clotted air of home;
And him again, and me again,
Another again like a hundred evenings,
Again misunderstood empty meanings,
Before sleep's cold relief.

Yet in the morning his fumbling gaze
Tugs the hemline of my ease.

And yes again, and yet again
I plan to leave and plan to leave
But again I turn back and take my keys,
My dreams too heavy when the day begins to wheeze—
(And they will whisper, "How my eyes are growing dim!")
My disappointment bulges in rolls around my chin
My flesh bloated and swollen as my hope grows ever thin—
(And they will whisper, "Oh she used to be so slim!")
And yet I plan
To stir the stale air.
One cold morning is enough
For a breeze or then a gale to blow away our worn affair.

But I have met this man already, met them all:
Have gone for dinner, drinks, the honeymoon,
I have drifted through my life on phony swoons;
I know his shows blaring through the flimsy walls
Drowning the lament of my heart torn and hewn.
      So how should we conclude?

But I have been alone already, been scalded raw—
I have blundered naked through their gaze,
Been wrapped tightly, squeezed and plastered with a grin,
When I am hung out for sale, bought and gnawed,
How will I set my chin
To scare the jackals off my last scraps, braised, ablaze?
        So why should we conclude?

But I have cast his heart already, cracked and flawed—
A heart I forged with hurt's bitter flare
(But in a desperate moment still a useful ware!)
Was it the inferno in my own chest
That fired hard our loneliness?
My heart, burned and frozen, freezer-burned and thawed
        So how should this conclude?
        And how should I forgive?

*   *   *   *   *   *   *

I could confess, I have stumbled out in the alleys of night's storm
Let the rain knot my hair as it tumbles from the eaves
Washing me in the rooftop's grime, the thick sediment of the city…

I could have waited for one of day's glittering puddles
And fluttered like a magpie to it's rippling edge.

*   *   *   *   *   *   *

And the evening, the night, turn so sleeplessly!
Churned by restless feet,
Raw… exhausted… indiscrete,
Spread across our bed, heavy with humidity.

Will I, after another sleepless night,
Have the nerve to start our final fight?
But though I have grown tough and bitter, tough and resolved,
Though I have convinced myself I want to see your head brought in upon a platter,
I am not Herodias—but a wife of Sodom and Gomorra;
I will resign my freedom to my nostalgia,
And I will sacrifice my future for some long forgotten pleasure,
And will stand frozen, crystallized like salt.

And would it have made any difference, any difference at all,
After wiping the sleep from my bleary eyes,
After hiding in the bathroom again to cry,
Would things have worked out any better,
If I had lied and said it didn't matter,
If I had swallowed my longing and said nothing at all.
If I had ingested this thought and let it fester,
Instead of saying: "I am Lot's wife, frozen stiff,
Turned away from you, turned away from it all"—
If I had not turned to you and spit
      With venom: "You never listen to me at all;
      You never listen, at all."

And would it have made any difference, any difference at all,
Would things have worked out any better,
After the sleepless nights and muffled crying in the bathroom,
After the biblical metaphors and making up and twisted sheets—
After these conversations and our little deceits—
You still never listen to anything I say!
But my nerves dissolved when your shattered face turns grey:
Would things have worked out any better.
If I had rubbed my eyes, smiled, and said nothing at all,
Instead of welling up with venom and spitting:

"You never listen at all,
You never listen to me, at all."

*　　*　　*　　*　　*　　*　　*

No! I am not Queen Gertrude, nor could I hope to be;
I am the Chamberlain's mild daughter, but I amuse the prince
I sway to his plot, happy to deliver his turns and twists,
Slight and sweet, there to be spurned or kissed,
Delirious, hysterical under crisis,
My flowers strewn carelessly yet still apologetic;
My frantic dance, foolish if not frenetic;
At times, indeed, they think me pathetic—
And yet, I could drown their distaste.

I am alone… and still alone…
I burry my desire in the marrow of my bones.

How to smooth my wrinkles out? Do I dare face the day's sickly heat?
I wait for night's forgiving darkness and then stroll along the streets.
I have heard the ravens calling, each to each.

I do not think they will call to me.

I watch them preening their black feathers in the treetops
Then spreading their wings to catch the night's breeze
When the wind's rough breath begins to wheeze.

We have floated on the currents of evening's air
With raven's iridescent feathers floating on the squall
Till dawn soothes the night's wind, and we fall.

WHAT IS POETRY? (A TWELVE-TONE POEM)
Susan Holbrook

trite yap show
rosy twit heap
posterity haw
a wept history
it's yawp rot, eh
a wisher potty
a power shitty
a whitey sport

poetry is what
whips yo tater
pets it awry, oh
oh, twisty pear
two hearts yip
it's paw theory

hi! try wet soap

ear whist typo
ape with story
or what ye spit
or what yeps it

throaty wipes
or what I types

WHAT IS PROSE
Susan Holbrook

Prose has wit,
war, hot spies,
pirate shows.
It has powers.
A swisher top,
wiser pathos,
towers, a ship,
parishes. Two
IHOPs. Waters
whose traps I
sap, so whiter
whites. Spa or
showier taps
spew hot airs:
"Poet wash, Sir?"
Posh waiters
tow Sharpies,
shower pitas,
pestos awhir,
pastries, how!

How it spears
trophies, was
tops, was heir
to Sears. "Whip
Thor, asswipe!
Swap heros!" it
whispers to a
hipster. Aw. So
worship a set.

WITHOUT YOU
Susan Holbrook

I wander lonely as a clod
in a bondless ble sky.
I'm living in a bbble,
the little engine
that cold.

I miss being a nit.

Me and my big
moth, devoring
every planet y'all
were in. Only
Mars and Earth
can sstain life now.
What a clsterfck!

I've lost ten ponds.
I've been hiding in the
hose reading *The History
of Tom Jones, a Fondling.*
I need my fond pot back.

I am ardor's American
neighbor. At the la
grass skirts hla;
I slmp in a
mm.

I'm in the Salt.

I know I was sed
bt I miss that sing.

PROBES
Ken Hunt

Wayward voyagers
cast out from our lush harbours
glide over Titan.

Particles litter
their golden shells, pleas of Sol
infinitesimal.

Gloves hands assembled
these sterile machines with
gentle diligence.

Probes bathe in deep space
to capture faint snapshots of
icecaps made of wind.

One generation
monitors what another
began, each waving

like the parents of
wide-eyed offspring embarking
on dark odysseys.

PHAGE
Ken Hunt

three men drift
in the womb of a metallic
bacteriophage

this quiet myovirus
stalks an untouched orb
of cratered rock

a silo of circuitry separates
from its quadruped partner
in this pressurized waltz
death craves a faltered step

descent reveals seas of pristine dust
and mountain ranges rough
with porous folds of rippled stone

horned rings of rock crown portals
to the tenebrous abyss
craters that cradle neither memory of
nor prophecy for life

what nether silence
shares the bulky shrouds
of explorers who tread
across night's dreaming eye

what palaces have shadows built

in the depths of Tycho and Neper
over solitary eons
as earth teemed and seethed with life

what black stars unhinge light
as we stumble through space

what minds hum
in contemplation
of our worth

IN THE SHADOW OF THE MOON
FOR BUZZ ALDRIN
Ken Hunt

I was open-minded
in anticipation watching
the earth grow smaller
the moon grow larger

but all of us were
totally surprised when
the larger moon
eclipsed the sun

we were in the shadow of the moon

satisfactory photographs
unfortunately
were not produced

the black sky was different
on the surface of the moon
from earth, the surrounding light
is visible when looking at the night sky

but on the surface of the moon
the sun's light gave
a pronounced velvet-like sheen
such that no stars were visible

the ambient light enabled stars

to be seen through the telescope
but not through the visor
cover on the eyes

THE UNICORN PARADE
Jani Krulc

This year, unicorns are everywhere and cupcakes are not yet dead (at least not for nine-year olds). I am in the kitchen stabbing unicorn tipped toothpicks into effervescently coloured cupcakes: Posh Blue, Raspberry Red (actually an enthusiastic magenta), We Love Yellow, and Dream Land (pale pink). The colours belie their flavours, which are simple vanillas and, in Posh Blue's case, chocolate. Unicorn-patterned crepe paper wraps itself up my bannisters and unicorn-plastered balloons hover inches from the ceiling, and the girls, their foreheads festooned with Etsy-ordered unicorn horns, run feral, unsupervised, beneath the bay window. The girls are unconcerned that underneath the horns their hair will become dented and plastered. They are still children.

No, they are unicorns.

I started the party with a game, I wrote the trivia questions myself, and gathered the girls around me in a semi-circle. Delilah, my birthday girl, sat in the centre of her minions, wearing a purple dress with chiffon skirt and multiple pink ribbons. The girls, who, as soon as their parents bid goodbye, began shrieking and running around my living room, shaking my daughters' presents and throwing the pillows I had arranged for them to sit on, were now immediately bored. Absently, they petted the lambskin rug and dropped small chins into small palms and sighed. One of them, Reagan, sucked on her hair, thoroughly soaking a strand before moving on to the next one, twisting the hair so that the ends resembled a paint brush, and then tucking it into the side of her mouth. Her top, patterned with red and blue hearts, was marked with wet blotches. Delilah, however, was eager and attentive, and she clapped her hands together and all her little friends perked up.

"Okay," I said, clearing my throat. "Which was the only animal not to make it onto Noah's ark?"

The girls gaped at my question and Delilah frowned.

Merla raised her hand.

"We don't believe in Noah's ark in my family," she said. "We believe in Darwin."

Then Chester, a little blonde girl with a stuffed nose said, "God made all the animals, every single one, and you and me."

Silence until Philippa, in a small voice said, "I know." She hesitated and then shouted "UNICORNS!" The girls erupted and whooped and began a chant, "Unicorns! Unicorns!"

I stood and waved my arms and bellowed, "Who wants a horn!" The girls ran towards me, hands grasping, and I held the horns above their heads and said "Simmer down." I handed out the horns, a gold-spackled deluxe thirty-dollar version for Delilah, and pastel papier mâché for the girls. They dispersed, galloping into the backyard, where they remain.

Georgina, a.k.a. helicopter parent numero uno, volunteered early on to help with the party.

"I'll herd," she said.

All us moms rely on Georgina's fear that Reagan, her daughter, the hair sucker, will die. Georgina volunteers for every field trip, book fair, and, best of all, every birthday party (in fact, would Reagan receive half the invitations she does without her mother's neurosis?). And I sympathize, really. I remember the time Delilah, age three, trundled out of sight on her red tricycle, flower-shaped bell happily pinging away, and, as soon as she crested the hill, a crash and a scream. Or her disappearance, age five, at Planet Organic, the paging over the intercom, me running from aisle to aisle, and at one point clasping the lapels of a stock boy who would find her napping on a bag of Kashi in the cereal aisle.

But fear infects Georgina's heart and mind and soul. Each morning, she stands beside the car and waves goodbye as Reagan skitters off. She waves until Reagan has entered the building and then her classroom. I have witnessed Georgina slink up to that classroom window and peer in. If Georgina were here today, she could peek outside, watch the girls to make sure no one pulls a pony tail or skins a knee. She could wipe down a counter or two, set the table, call the pizza place, perhaps organize goody bags. She could help facilitate the other games I planned, such as,

- Pin the horn on the unicorn
- Musical unicorn chairs
- Unicorn, who stole your magic pouch?

But yesterday, at school pick-up, Georgina announced that she could not attend the party after all, that her therapist felt she was spending too much time on other people's needs. Her therapist had, in fact, ordered her to spend a day at the spa.

"I'm sorry Elaine, but you understand." Her finely-lined upper lip (Reagan was an IVF baby) quivered. "Dr. Gerald says I need more me time or my adrenals will never recover."

Thank God for cupcakes. Last year when fairies were all the rage and all the girls inexplicably wore tutus, I baked a cake. At the last minute the belly of the cake collapsed in on itself and all the cream frosting in the world couldn't hide its anemic centre. The candles drowned in the soft sugar. Delilah took one look and oh the tears. Eight little girls experiencing schadenfreude for the first time rustled after Delilah into her bedroom. I could not coax them out of the room but Chris, hero daddy Chris, returned from Dairy

Queen with an ice cream cake and even elicited from our petulant little princess a hug for mom, the cake destroyer.

Later she said, "I was so embarrassed," and Chris placed a palm on her soft hair and tickled her chin until she laughed.

Should I have said to a freshly-turned eight-year-old child that my own eighth birthday party was crashed by an obese Greek cousin named Yiorgos, who claimed the paddle pool and sloshed out half the water? He refilled the pool while lying in it, the hose's nozzle a perverse underwater gusher, and when the pool was full, Yiorgos held the limp hose over his face and let the water soak his hair. His stomach, a perfectly round island emerged from the water, burned bright red, the belly button stretched into a surprised O. Yiorgos ate a piece of cake the size of a baby and opened the second bucket of ice cream and spooned and spooned and then drank the liquid cream at the bottom of the bucket.

"Mom, mom, mom, when is the pizza going to be ready?" Delilah's bow of a mouth is stained red from the cherry candy one of her friends has smuggled in. They all stare at me, ten pairs of unpainted eyes. They smell young and fresh, like little puppies.

"I have ordered the pizza. It will be here in thirty minutes." My body hides the cupcakes. They have snuck up on me, one minute wildlings, the next stealth raiders.

"But we're so hungry!" The girls retreat, moaning, clutching their stomachs.

I arrange the nine candles on Delilah's over-sized tri-coloured birthday cupcake.

Outside, the girls roll their Rs and ululate. Trilling, they call it. When I ask, Delilah says, "Unicorns don't neigh, duh."

Fat cousin Yiorgos was all that the girls wanted to talk about the Monday after my party. We had one week left of school and it seemed we spent the entire time in unstructured activities, abandoned by our teachers.

"Your cousin, what's his name?"
"His name is so weird!"
"He eats so much!"
"Be careful he doesn't eat your cat!"
"How do you say his name?"
"Is everyone from your country so fat?"

My hands sweated their prints into the cloth cover of the book I was supposed to be reading.

The thing is, Missy's brother spent all his time in a wheelchair, his hands permanently pressed into bird claws. Sierra's mother had cancer and all her hair fell out, and she came to the Christmas concert with a yellow scarf tied around her scalp that slid off and landed in a puddle of slush in the parking lot. Aubrey's parents were divorced, and she saw her father only in the summers at a big lake in Ontario. She had a stepmom and three step siblings.

Before Yiorgos, nothing distinguished me. Perhaps my curly hair. But now I had a fat foreign cousin with an unpronounceable name.

"He's disgusting," I said. "I hate him."
"My mom said you shouldn't hate anyone, ever," Sierra said.
"My mom said the same thing," Missy said.

We toured Aunt Soula and Cousin Yiorgos around for two months, driving to the mountains and the dinosaur bones and BC, up and down the coast and then to the islands. In the fall, a new girl appeared at school, little Marissa with straight golden hair, and she joined the group, and suddenly, with me, there were five. I had to partner up with Augusta, a transplant from England, and my place with the other girls eroded by Halloween and then disappeared.

Delilah and her friends are playing in her room. They can try on her princess dresses and pop the heads off her Barbies and neigh/trill all they want, but I have hidden her FAO Schwartz teddy and the vintage porcelain doll from Paris. They do not hear the doorbell, which announces the pizza, all half dozen boxes. Not that the girls are such big eaters, but every second one has a dietary restriction: no pork (Rebecca – Jewish); no gluten (Penelope – on a diet, though her mother claims it's a sensitivity); no cheese (Aurora – legitimate dairy allergy); no fish (Reagan – Georgina's fear of mercury poison).

I set the table and arrange the pizzas on stone slabs so that they don't touch.

Chris is supposed to be here. He even canceled golf.

He is not. He is on a plane to Singapore, via Frankfurt. Last minute.

He took care of entertainment, though, which means his secretary made a few calls.

Delilah's door is unlocked. The girls, silent, kneel huddled around Violet, the Parisian doll, whose skull has split down the centre. Violet's eyes stare sideways, askance.

"Girls," I say. "What happened?" All ten of them tear up and sniffle. Delilah begins to whine, the precursor to a howl. I cut her off.

"Never mind," I say. "There's pizza."

They run off and I scoop up what is left of Violet, the two halves of her porcelain head still attached to her body.

My mother did not notice the diminishing number of birthday

party invitations I received, or, if she did, she considered it a blessing, fewer gifts to buy, fewer names to remember, fewer play dates to chaperone. By sixth grade, my old friends and I existed on separate planets, theirs the refuge of the petite and the popular, the flirtatious and the pretty. Mine was the realm of pre-menstrual cramps and budding breasts, abdominal fat that would not shift to my hips until high school, large feet and myopia.

    I consider my path the more righteous one, the path of pain and self-reflexivity, forced independence and eventual growth. I fear that Delilah, my elfin child with straight hair and big eyes and lithe limbs, will glide through the years of adolescence and even early adulthood unscathed, her character untested and soft.

None of the girls eat their crusts.
    "The pizza hurts our mouths! Am I bleeding?" Delilah opens her mouth, masticated crudo and arugula displayed on her tongue.
    "Who wants seconds?"
    "Cake!" Delilah shouts. "Cake!"
    The girls abandon their plates, their fizzy water and orange juice, and I run after them.
    "Stay in the living room, stay right here," I say. They look at me, eyes shining.

Lighting nine candles and dimming the chandelier and taking a picture at the same time is impossible.
    "Smile," I say.
    Delilah's little friends beam.
    "Mom, the candles are melting!"
    In the first photograph, Delilah pouts, her unicorn horn slipping onto her forehead, obscuring her eyes.

I beckon her to the kitchen.

"If you don't smarten up," I grab her arm and adjust her horn, "everyone is going home."

Her arms are so thin, just skin and bone like a chicken's neck. She ragdolls and sways.

"Stand up straight," I say. "What would your dad say if he were here?"

Some grandmothers attend, if not organize, their grandchildren's birthday parties. I did not know my own grandmother, she came from the same place as Yiorgos and Aunt Soula, a small village of two hundred that had only one phone for everyone, in the tobacco shop. Every two weeks I would spend a torturous few minutes (it felt like a lifetime) speaking to my weeping *yaiyai*, repeating the only Greek words I knew: *sa ga po*. I love you.

Delilah's grandmother, my mother, has settled in her own village in the west coast on an island. Near the ocean, she runs a B&B, which features a kiln, and potters and other artist types visit her from all over. It's hard for her to get away, she says, so she rarely does.

A wide enough smile and pearly teeth.

Six candles smoke, an enthusiastic gust, flame. Camera flash lights the room.

"Cake!" Delilah starts the chant. "Cake! Cake! Cake!" They grab the cupcakes without waiting for napkins. They march behind my daughter, sticky-palmed, crumbs the size of cockroaches dropping to the floor. They chant "Cake! Cake! Cake!" with mouths full.

The doorbell rings – Georgina? Save me, please. The children can't hear its peal, they march on through the living room and into the kitchen. I open the door as they come back into the foyer.

How could hero daddy Chris, devoted husband, know his child is terrified of clowns?

How could his secretary?

Cheerio the Creative Clown sports orange wig and checkered doctor's coat, with spoof stethoscope and cartoonishly large magnifying glass, like a terrifying gynecologist. Purple nose, white face, violet smile.

Delilah, mouth full of tri-coloured Queen Bee cupcake, freezes.

Cheerio shouts "Surprise!"

Delilah wets herself and I snap pictures, the other girls, delighted, clapping their hands, or hooves. They trill.

GOODBYE BUTTERFLY, HELLO KITTY: AN OPIATE OPERA
Larissa Lai

and homage to david bateman
with apologies to hiromi goto

riffing on the work of david bateman, hiromi goto, angela rawlings, david khang, henry tsang, fred wah, phinder dulai, jam. ismail, ajaykumar and other winged critters on unsanctioned flight paths

players
madame butterfly
hello kitty
a bust of the goddess athena
fed-ex pilot pinkerton
co-pilot goro
chorus
a voice

prologue
int. of a shipping container. dark. hour uncertain. a woman dressed in kitsch geisha gear, a hodgepodge of as many icons of asian femininity as set deck can muster, sits at an old fashioned vanity. propped up on the vanity is an alabaster bust of the goddess athena. on the other side of the emptied mirror frame sits another woman with a hello kitty mask over her head.

chorus:
butterfly bites back
dreams she is a man dreaming
woman dreaming eye
of owl on camouflage wing

butterfly:
multiples at discount bulks my purchase
the dress i saw on the maker's mannequin
the dress i sew my fingers so nimble quick
jacks a lantern
pattern patented at corporate
hq for gq et al.
my eyes sharp as needles' haystacks
you'll never find me
never mind neverland
i thread the eye as camels pass and angels dance
designer gesture
brushstroke zen in nyc while i move machinic
the seam seems
my gratitude so happy to host you
my seer sucker puckers
flaw foretells futures
gamble on interest spike
hearts of daytraders leap
at chance of my collective
market reaction
manufacture my desire
i buy ideas
work yarn   factory farm
open for business from zip to zatch
forensic evidence obvious as danger's

one per cent doctrine
love me love my dogma
organ banks pumps in a row
so dumb they don't get democracy
sweet cellular network
access online
broadband wireless tireless and
instantly available
endlessly interchangeable
this heart or that heart
break it replace it
they're all mine
leaking mercury into yellow river

chorus:
butterfly's hot for mothra
frantic mantra:
scale matters

butterfly:
i've swallowed a whale
engulfing that which engulfs me
will i be rescued by love?
virago sighs
dodging dragon's friendly fire
my i's teeth seed armies
faithful to nation
stationed in territory
terror mirrors

i become what i accuse
through my longing for lemonade

and baked alaska
the master enters
i am his house
seeking the tools of my own destruction

alien autopsy
my unheimlich familiar
here kitty kitty
hello pussy's poker-faced palace
vs. our athena
busting open her father's head
with a war-like cry

athena:
thank-you mr. clean
for your lemon fresh scent
my floors sparkle
the mythic mess of archetype's
bloody drama
mucks your bucket

act 1, scene 1
int. of a moving container
hour uncertain

butterfly:
i get it, man, you tricked me
but i've already dreamt your dream
i forget what i was before
stuck in your taxonomy with you

my outside's inside-out
often pregnant
my kitty, my athena
they're just the start

hello kitty:
don't start with me,
pussy-face, don't you know
i was made in your image? it's dark in here
and i never asked
to be shipped in this container
what's that smell?
i miss my litter box.

bust of athena:
reason, ladies, reason.
there's got to be one for this dark,
these walls. i think we're at sea
because of the way the box rocks.
what do you think it says on the outside
worker? martyr? illegal migrant? sensual massage?

butterfly:
i wanted, i wanted
all i wanted was
want
wanted the white girl
in the white dress
wanted the white house with the white curtains
billowing in the cool breeze
blowing through a white window frame
above a winter white garden

with the frothy sea capped in white waves
down below

bust of athena:
to be or to have?

butterfly:
i wanted the want
to be the want, to have the want
to be wanted
i was a walking want ad
petite asian lady
dark hair pale-skin
perhaps a little oversensitive
seeks white man with white house
seeks white woman with white teeth
seeks elephant tusk ivory seeks white sale
lovely linen sheets and quilt covers
seeks thread count seeks egyptian cotton
seeks expensive intensive
seeks lifestyle, seeks lifeboat
i wanted help
what does a woman want
when she's a butterfly dreaming she's a man?

bust of athena:
to have then.

butterfly:
no! to be and not to be
i lost my or, i threw it away
and went adrift

a long time ago
before you were born
from your father's head
i wanted to be
the dream fulfilled

bust of athena:
whose dream?

butterfly:
there's the rub a dub dub
three men in a tub
all dreaming they are butterflies
my cocoon's multiple
orgasmic as many flavours as robin
hood basking in the light
of revolution digital
miniscule my tiny agile hands
the electronic industry's so hungry for

bust of athena:
i'm here for the class war
the pasture
never mind my noble birth
i'm here for intel
outside your microprocessor accelerates
my fury
don't get mad
get leavened bread
the wrong people are fasting
the revolution will be stigmatized
ideologized by anchors and wankers

don't ask my father
about truth in advertising
he ate my mother

kitty:
they were such cannibals before i was born
consumers consuming consumers consuming consumers
its only because they didn't understand oligopoly
the concentration of power into the hands of even fewer
trumps and blacks and back door hacks
take another little piece of my harp
i never pretended to be an angel
so cute i can't stand the mirror
rebel without a pause
brand without commodity
i'm pure concept
and i'm here to take your daughters

butterfly:
only those with bodies get boxed
we could cut free of our containers
but i'm so attached

athena:
samsara sera

there is a knock on the outside of the container

athena:
who's there?

a voice:
orange

athena:
orange who?

voice:
orange county, china
next stop

butterfly:
we haven't got nearly as far as i'd hoped
shouldn't we be in america by now?

voice:
don't be so twentieth century
location's vocation is a lost art
information passed real estate's power hour
on the autobahn of a swan song
your tea's opium traded by mandarin's minions
the orange's clockwork long since
analyzed and reproduced
sourcing the boot of fascism's distant longings

kitty:
i think he's saying we've already been to america
and now we're on our way back

athena:
around the world in one long boxed night

kitty paws the ground in frustration

kitty:
my mimicry licks disney
who needs a german fairytale when you can do it

on pure marketing savvy
my graphic stops traffic
my honour stockpiles key chains and coin purses
pendants, t-shirts, mini-skirts
muffs, powder puffs, socks, stockings,
gameboys, notepads
later they gave me my own credit card
my buying power sticks it
to cricket's wicket
the lonely colonial
left nursing his last stand
let me out of this box

a crack of light appears momentarily in the ceiling and a lap top tumbles through the hole

voice:
here's a key
to unlock your longing

bust of athena:
that's mine. i'm the brains around here.

butterfly:
i'm brawn, pure labour power at your service
and the only pair of hands in the room

kitty examines her paws and looks disgruntled. butterfly flips the lid of the laptop. to the surprise of all three players, it is also a projector. a windows xp screensaver flashes up on the far wall of the container. butterfly googles herself, comes up with various images of herself, devastated or dying against japonesque backgrounds.

this tragic outfit is such a drag
hag begs fresh narrative
non-drowsy medication for a new asian nation

kitty:

produces a compact, the back of which is her own face

flush with stuff for co-prosperity
against austerity
here's a mirror to cover your other
a new same to name your difference

athena:
lesson in the pardon
capital's garden trademarks happiness
hordes of buddhas
jam freeways
rock to ipods
in green hummers

butterfly:
want to pave my empire against american cash
and war the store of anti-asiatic actions
my caption can't read
peace

athena:
breaking up is hard to do
drop your old threads
you could be handed any old hand-me-down
hounds of hell or love
a covey of done and dusted doves

irish rovers
russell stover chocolates
a moving van's sun tan tailored
for the snowbird masses
packaging holidays in puerto vallerta
shouldn't you be a little more careful?

butterfly:
check this site
lonely man seeks sweet petite
to add raunch to southern alberta ranch
what a chance
i can dance
if i wanna

kitty:
if you're gonna sell out
don't sell flesh
sell the master his own narrative
comparative sedative
repetitive and competitive as mass-produced mirrors
targetting walmart and hallmark
millions of sentimental journeys before the final gurney
cheap labour conquering the world

athena:
hands that launch a thousand quips
the flip of western consumption
the gumption of production
execute the officer
seize control of coffers swollen
with stolen loot

while butterflies flood factories
and monsanto terminates rice and rape
the scorn of corn
abandoning indigenes for meat and bun

kitty:
does this seem a face that cares?
my plastic gaze can stare down
all but the most immortal ceos
my replication guarantees
my continuation in perpetuity
i'm here and i'm there
i'm just and unfair
i'm gonna live forever
now let's trade this mirror
and see what we can get

butterfly:
bidding's begun
curse of your worth
caught in the purses of young women
and middle-aged men
pitching projections
sweet, cute, floozy or sleazy
whatever sauce your gander genders
gesture of jesters
fluster busted
by how i love
a man in uniform

kitty:
your unicorn's pre-teen duty
the cock in asian
the cut in cute
if a metaphor is split
in a pome
do trees fall in forests?

athena:
as long as mac blows canfor
and feds collude
the rude rumble of chainsaws
gains old growth
and our asian yells timber
to rise from the ashes
of revolutions' missed mark

butterfly:
i marked the mirror
'personally inscribed'
your worth is rising

kitty:
not surprising
the world market is my troy
and i don't need no horse-face
to take it down for me
this is war girls
and i'm not gonna stop
til i rule every last bull and bear

athena:
your chinashop stops all teapots
porcelain to opium
walkman, intel, bluetooth
the parking booth
our phine phriend
phones home from

butterfly:
the auction closes in three days
and we'll need a post office
or the fed ex man
have i told you how i love…

athena:
i know
the dove of peace
or at least
a good night's sleep

EYE
Naomi K. Lewis

When I was a boy, fourteen or sixteen, my parents moved us to the prairies. They called it "God's kingdom." They meant that literally. It was a religion they'd joined.

I was a stranger to the colonies, as we still thought of them then, though technically the empire was already long defunct, and I had never, in all my short life, entertained the slightest notion of leaving the great city of my birth, once the centre of the civilized world. On these prairies, we lived in what passed for a city. I began crashing my bicycle into every bit of God's kingdom I could find. After a few less dramatic smash-ups, I sped into a statue of two businessmen conversing on the pavement. I launched over my handlebars and into their arms. The plaintive one with the briefcase had two fingers raised, to emphasize a point. Which was how I got this scar on my neck, how I became disillusioned with religion, and how I ended up estranged from my parents and living on my own in the wild west by the age of seventeen-and-a-half.

You would not believe how many people said to me, back then, "You're lucky you didn't lose an eye." And that was five years before I met my first wife, Lila.

When my second wife said she was leaving me, you know what I told her? I said that if she expected to see me broken hearted, she was in for a disappointment. I said I was too old for that kind of thing. I was thirty-two. That's a bit of a private joke for me these days, because, of course, I am broken hearted now, and a whole lot older than thirty-two, though I won't say by how much. My currently broken heart is what's prompted me to tell you all this. The point is, after what happened with my first wife, my heart was such a collection of shards and smithereens that breaking it again was out of the question for some decades. The other point is, life is long, and a second instance of heartbreak feels entirely different from a first.

So, Lila. Like most people, she talked about her childhood; hers had transpired in a forest by a lake.

"We tapped the trees, and we had so much maple syrup, we used to fry our eggs in that instead of oil."

"Did you ever pour it on the snow to make candy?" said me.

"Yes."

Incredible, I know. How could a child privy to that much syrup – who squeaked her little boots under towering mid-continent maples, collecting buckets of sap from the tapped trunks, who boiled it down in one of those giant cauldrons, standing in the cold, breathing the sugary steam; how could she go and grow into her twenties to be such a, excuse me but, cunt?

Me and Lila, we were never married; no, not in the sense of being legally married. But I've always thought of her as my first wife, and for a number of compelling reasons. Number one, because she pulverized my heart. Number two, because I gave her my eye. Number three, because after she left, I stood in the snow outside her trailer. If nights find you standing in the wispy prairie-snow outside the trailer of your ex-wife, it's that some part of you is still in there, and you're drawn back to it, the way a ghost is stuck haunting the site of its murder; but if that trailer belongs to someone you were never married to in the first place, that makes you a stalker. I can tell you for certain, I was no stalker.

I know what you're thinking: My eye?

It began with a wish I made in the heat of passion. We'd been out dancing and drinking and sweating and smelling each other's sweat while we danced. Then back at her place we're already kissing on the stairs, throwing each other against the walls, and then, finally through her apartment door, shedding clothes on our way to the bed. (That's right; she lived in an apartment on the third story of a house. Not in a trailer. We lived in what passed for a city, and she lived in an apartment in a house, and when I would stand in the snow at night, it would be in the small gap between Lila's house and the one next door.)

I said, "I wish your organs would fail so I could prove how much I love you. I wish I could give you my lung, my kidney, a piece of my liver. Some part of me working inside your body, its vessels pumped through with your blood."

"That's a weird thing to wish," said Lila.

"I would do it, I promise you. It would be a tattoo of my name, only more so. A hundred times more so." All the while, I traced my fingers over her bare skin and mine, imagining where the incisions would be.

I know what you're thinking. But those are the kinds of things we say when our hearts are young and plump and dented only by the unwilling move across an ocean to a land of interminable wheat fields and jarred cheese. Even the loss of a country with millennia of culture can't compare to the loss of a twenty-three-year-old's first love, a rosy-nippled woman with black fruity-smelling hair. And eyes – well, eyes that started out nut-brown, but were destined to be green with brown rings around the pupils, exactly like mine. Not *like* mine. Mine.

My dear Helen, who of course I lost just recently after thirty brief years, found it deeply disturbing that someone, Lila, namely, was walking around out there with my eye in her head. (The word 'deeply' was a bit of private joke between Helen and me since depth is exactly what you can't perceive after giving away one eye.) What bothered Helen most was the scene in the hospital, which she sometimes dreamed about, though she hadn't been there of course and only had what I'd told her to go on – the doctor peeling the bandage from around Lila's head, and she on the exam table, blinking into my face with my very own eyeball now wired to her cortex.

Lila opened my eye wide and we examined each other – real eye to glass eye, glass eye to real eye.

"I'm just not sure I love you, though, Hank," she said. "My sense of love feels kind of empty."

If I had been older at the time, I'd have known the Hank thing was a bad sign all along. She called me that because she thought it was a suitable name for someone who wore plaid shirts, drove a pickup truck, and had a big black dog. I did none of those things. But she kept calling me Hank, hoping the shirt, truck, and four-legged companion would follow. I told her I was born abroad; I showed her the scar on my neck. I repeated my given name. She was not convinced.

Does it seem strange that so soon after losing Helen, I'm telling the story of Lila and my eye, instead the story of Helen and my life? That I want to explain how we were fighting when the accident happened? We were driving beside a spruce grove on one side and a canola field on the other, and I wanted Lila to turn into the yellow and stop the car so I could work myself up into her skirt. Like she'd let me do a year before.

"Give me, give me."

"No, no, no."

"Your breasts. Your mouth. Your underwear around your ankles."

"No."

"Why, why, Lila!"

"I don't love you I don't love you!"

I grabbed; she shoved. Her other arm wrenched the wheel away from bright paradise and into the cool dark trees. Smashed glass, little jewels of it, the branch in the car, blood everywhere. Most of it hers. Two weeks later, I got the test; I was a donor. I came to, and my eye socket wasn't empty, but brim bursting with pure agony. Is it too obvious to point out that having your eye removed and your heart ripped out hurts? Some things are describable, that's all, and some things aren't. I'm telling you what I can.

HAND-IN-HAND
(FOR DAPHNE MARLATT)
Nicole Markotić

i
won hundred
goest werx

how belatedly we late we
: a sample (plus one, plus ample ease)

trine moods, dining meds, a skip off the curb-drop
a best in the stopper

\ mush goes awnings
ghat isn't?

bleem between friends
    or thyme in yr sammich

ecks sells lends
wi wouldn't she?

eyeliner winddays
pro or miss holi fogs

chat's about all, fox
jo*y

and a haf;ful
often or offen

bees cause their own demi-sasse
) he's adam; he's this ant

gents rate shins
mow or rest = exactamundo

jolt#
withheld(as used

for beg,s for plé
asterisks, the comet

eleven times Vancou!er marrs late hystery
 tah-dah

ii
sel electrons 4
   re-re-ing mar's latter dash

sirs stain slots
slurs retain, often after

networthing
pre ends the plop

a hub risk, a vali
cinse to sentz

bly a brick in the upper thugs
tranting. now. few

integers for four times
a matrix of wow. new

slap-stick and spastic
gerunding

runcible marx @mark
tell hunched | tell tweyes

izn teas props for mercy
a hearse and a curb8 fayn

tenting
a finale to the key

rakes a channel
    x-teen

twell forbite
a deeming and a dron't

reeks incensed
    sleventeen

e-mind the hobo-gap
a twisent" a pince of the sol^ a momunto blingk on the rizon; sen

iii
burb packing, a lasso of poscipality
rainoe

forge treks bekum
ecksakta belds

blend in wit the dime of the see-sow
it habn't, they dunay. trithe

werkily down, a bout ovten
astardly, garts, and entimole

now's not the framework, now's ow-ing
owe too, one toe

thenk and tri-little these fore bayds
a yenkin. Strice

devlon trips to cascading
a worry ; a wirth ; a tuscero

likely or gabillion
same mem

iv doesn?t
as if when se much songs ta wen

twiss more than tether
ballpark Layers

rightyho & yo$
6

the famished-line finish
matches afling

go singe the top bluster
yes > yes

one blood
and again: this isn't the @app

CRAWLEY HALL
(EXCERPT FROM NOVEL-IN-PROGRESS)
Suzette Mayr

You are a tower you are cells in a hive of industrial tile and asbestos, concrete, steel pipe, iron rebar skeleton. You are bathroom doors dangling off their hinges you are sputtering fluorescent lights you are elevators noosed and suspended between floors. You are silverfish and mould, you are spores and condensation trickling down windows, inside walls. You are drywall and dust. You are blackening beams. You are leaky ceilings you are stuffed with fibre glass, sharp and cotton candy. You are styrene, formaldehyde, butoxyethanol, phthalate, you are offices with no windows at all. You are a woman who has locked herself in a cleaning supply closet, who scrabbles her fingers along the edges of the doorframe, waiting for someone to remember her. You murmur, breathe in your own stale air, air redolent with concrete and decay. The woman turns away from the doorframe, faces into the room. Thumps her head back against the concrete wall. Waiting. Her phone shines a light so pale it turns her whole body blue. You are bones. You are tissue.

You are another woman shuffling papers in her office, shunting papers and books from one stack to another to another, building a wall in front of her, walls behind her. You are her headache. You are that odd smell slithering from the heating vent, you are that rigidness in the women's lungs, you are that feeling that they are sinking, have sunk up to her mouth, and soon you will be closing in over their noses. You are concrete you are iron you are wood you are plastic you are drywall you are bones and buttons and shreds of cloth you are molecules crumbling you are sputtering, leaking, dissolving.

UNHOLD FIENDS
AFTER SEBASTIAN BIENIEK'S "DOUBLE FACED" SERIES
kevin mcpherson eckhoff

genial gift

parole

bang

puff

      after, rumpf

fast brand,

qualm

spur

gully

        hang

bad

rat

ringer

die

        bald

          tripper

        fade

apart

stapler

pendant

labor

tier

lack

      art

see, wand

        provision

quote

quark

dose

handy

      war

mist

ON ANATOMICAL PROCEDURES
Sandy Pool

I think I am a nice person, but then, I think, maybe not. As it turns out, 52% of my acquaintances believe I am a nice person, while 11 % believe I am a moderately nice person. 6% believe I am rarely a nice person, and the rest refused to answer the questionnaire. Out of the 52% of people who think I am a nice person, 87% of them believe that I would give up my seat to an elderly person on the bus. However, only 14% believe that I would give them one of my kidneys, if medically necessary, and only 43% believe that I am nice to my mother. 92% of this group believe they are nice people, with 81% believing they are nicer than I am. Out of the 11% who believe I am a moderately nice person, 61% believe that I am nice on certain occasions, and not nice on other occasions. The occasions included dinner parties, hospitals, baby christenings, weddings, and laundromats. However, due to a mistake in the survey composition, the participants did not specify which occasions I was nice at. Out of the 6% who believe I am rarely a nice person, almost 80% suggest that I am nicer to them when I have consumed 1-2 glasses of unspecified alcohol. 90% suggest that I am subsequently nicer when I have consumed 3-4 glasses of unspecified alcohol. 63% of this group also believes that I have a drinking problem. Unfortunately, I cannot account for those who refused to answer the questionnaire, so I can only imagine what they must think of me.

ONE STRAND AT A TIME
Sharanpal Ruprai

Every morning, a disciplined choice of a black starched turban.
Dreams of combing fingers through short black hair vanish
every morning. In front of an open locker
an inspection for unruly strands.
Bullies yell down the hall *ride them' cowgirls!*
Avoid eye-contact and stare at yourself in the mirror.

In the washroom, a fist into a mirror.
Every morning, a disciplined bully trashes a turban
avoid gym, too hot and sweaty to play tag and cowgirls
do not care for brown skinned cowboys.
                                     Dreams of track'n field gold vanish
Parents think, a bookish child, good thing really. Strands
of rope tucked away in a locker.

Down the hall a push into the open locker
a click of a lock, a scream, *let me out,* a mirror
shatters and unruly strands
poke out and bullies pull at an unravelled turban
Dreams of making it through the day unharmed vanish.
bullies yell *heehaw heehaw, ride them' cowgirls!*

No more heehaw or ride them'cowgirls!
No more being shoved into a locker.
Dreams of short black hair vanish.
A pair of scissors, black elastic, a mirror
and a hacked up turban,
in the school bathroom long black strands.

Snip one strand, snip two strands, snip three strands
of hair hacked up all over the floor, no more cowgirls
taunts, no more dirty turban
lover jokes, no more being thrust into a locker
a sneer in the mirror
a sneer, tears and fear in the mirror vanish.

They gawk, we gawk, parents gawk
                              and dreams of a good Sikh child, vanish.
Tears stream and hair strands
are stuck to the school bathroom mirror.
Students cowered in the gym. No brave cowgirls
anymore, police, principal, and parents peer into a locker
the murder weapon is longer than a turban.

Every morning, in front of a locker, the sounds of snipping strands
In the school bathroom a turban cowgirl
vanishes in the mirror.

THE TALE OF PINUCCIO AND NICCOLOSA
(AFTER THE ITALIAN OF GIOVANNI BOCCACCIO)
Ian Sampson

So ends the tale of Calandrino,
who made the crowd buzz
like a giddy neutrino,

and again they'd buzz
when one of the women, a *mafiosa*,
bid Panfilo tell a tale, which was:

"Get this. Niccolosa,
not the love of Calandrino –
there's another Niccolosa

who lived by the casino
her father owned in the valley
of Mugnone, serving *vino*

locale to pilgrims who rally
on the highway to Rome –
Niccolosa, yes, a hot tamale,

still at home
at sixteen, with a brother
(age two) and a mother to comb

her curls, or sew muslin to smother
her curves. Enter a libertine
from Florence (a smoother

operator she'd never seen)
who caught her gaze, cocksure,
as she nibbled a tangerine

and made him heartsore
under his white shirt
(Armani, our man wore).

So they'd flirt:
she dropped her wimple for Prada
and a skirt

that flashed like an armada
aflame. First date (his grotto):
dancing lambada

to the tap of her stiletto,
he let her swoop: "I love you,"
he said and she said, "Ditto."

She'd undo him impromptu
but the man,
Pinuccio, to cushion her virtue,

ad-libbed a plan:
he called a cab for the damsel
then he got his sedan

tanked up with diesel
and buffed the autobody
like Bellini at an easel;

and he revved the Maserati
with an air of irreverence
and cruised the autostrada

out of Florence.
Adriano, his crony, rode shotgun.
They let the cadence

of the engine run
shrill, pulled up to the motel
by the last threads of sun

and rang the doorbell.
Her father, a kind of underboss,
offered Zinfandel

and Calvados
(both contraband) to get them buzzed
and mumbled like a contrabass.

Old news: the casino's bust;
the boss'll rent his cozy home
to cozen florins from his guest.

Double bed with memory foam
and meals are free, veal ravioli
by the gastronome

at seven, with lemon aioli
and a tumbler of rum
to purge the *E. coli.*

Imagine their home: one room,
two beds by one wall, one by the other,
and slim as a catacomb;

Niccolosa alone, her mother
and father by the baby's crib,
the lodgers together.

When night fell, he slid glib
out of bed, Pinuccio,
and glid to his girl to put his lip

to hers, livid with libido,
and made love (his forte)
incognito.

Let the *commedia dell'arte*
begin: a cat toggled (with a forepaw)
the pianoforte;

the mother got up to draw
the curtain and see what's amiss;
Adriano, by Murphy's Law,

was out to piss
and groping back to bed, the crib in his way,
shifted it from their side to his.

She, still in negligée,
rejoined her man, or the man
she took for hers amid the disarray

of an altered floor-plan
and slipped under his arm
(Adriano's) his courtesan.

Pinuccio, his charm
spent, afraid to be caught with a coed
by the gendarme

or his wife, went to bed
and got cozy
in a quilt he thought his, misled

by the crib. "Niccolosa,"
he said, "I frigged her like a knave
in a tome of *curiosa*."

And held his breath a semibreve
when a hand fiddled at his throat.
"Fear me, Casanova; I'm the reeve

that fed you, and you gloat
you glut your urges on my girl.
Why not dote

on her with daffodils, or snip a curl
from her wimple?
To rob her of her pearl,

Pinuccio, is death." Atremble,
the lover bluffed: "What now?"
(As a barrel fondled his temple.)

"What *now*?"
said the boss.
"I'll tell you what now.

I get medieval on your ass
with a waterboard and holy water
blessed at High Mass."

To thwart slaughter,
the mother, like a mute belladonna,
moved to her daughter.

"Bemoan no Desdemona,
husband: you're drunk,
and croon Corona

by the bubble. Our girl's in the bunk
I've huddled in all night.
So tell me who's the hunk

propped upright
by your elbow with a brow more blotto
than Snow White?"

"My bro," said Adriano,
"he dreams he's Cupid
in a nude by Watteau

and wanders rigid
in his sleep. Rub an ember
on his palm, he'll lift an eyelid.

Limp as if from slumber
(or from rum), Pinuccio woke
and feigned to not remember

his dream. They broke
bread over custard blended
from egg yolk

and the offended
sipped a cup of espresso:
all's mended.

So *recto* turned to *verso*:
they paid up in florins
and fueled up with Esso

without interference
and drove the Maserati
into Florence,

tasting victory (or was it Bacardi?).
As they blinked out of view,
Niccolosa recalled her lover's body,

on hers, a preview of a rendezvous
to come. Or like Carmela Soprano,
when the cat (*déjà vu*)

pawed a tune on the piano,
her mother dreamt of Adriano."

DAWN (FROM THE DAY BOOK)
Jordan Scott

Variable irradiance; variable background. Body in sun beyond the shadow of a doubt. Buoyant reflectance; bouillon carbon. Good soil lights up lit-up hands carbon of so much work. Light, neither-here nor-there, wondering glow nestle liquid scree. Somewhere perfect heat; perfectly real and concrete; perfect soluble forms perfect no more. Shore heat; shored-up up by eternities of faith, and crumble puffs of ice-dust come fair and sharing-off light and shade. Come here, fair bodies. Fair says the world to come, says displaced color starts here, one with another - first melt - then leak - first painting: "Say, look at that quivering landscape." Of a body, the remarkableness of it all, display against all other bodies. Firm heat; infirm sun. Clarity comes after: "Say, see the moon in morning."

Dawn is the drawing of a line – one made with a finger across water, hands across the back of an animal, several fingers through a lover's hair – see anxious landscape; see light advance - error of pen mark from rib to ear. Who has faith in the arbitrary? But in our sun and what it covers. This loneliness. Remains. This country. I want the sun to cover everything. Nape itself; limbs hard-site; what wraps together as skin? My rock to your hard place. Then bit by bit, a touching of everything. Everything is interesting. A man against a tree, an obstacle in front of a lizard. An octopus draped atop a whale. A mountain and a glacier. Our simple heads, last drenched - last glow animal praxis; glow our path into solemn etcera.

It becomes bright. There is nothing more to do. It's all I've ever wanted.

Ambrosian animal snout; sun receptacle passing species; simply living yet so taken by food; so taken with sweetness. All bees, you are, simply taken by food, and given subtle bodies, given subtle matter, who would not wonder at a chameleon in our midst?

We have need of light that will bring fulfillment. Light our being, our matter, and mercy in shadow's cold movements downwards, as in the case of water, as in what is visible, congealing as foam or phlegm - all sick - to learn, that is, to know, the gem hidden in the phenomena of color.

Pink-purple green-yellow red-purple inches of tan-yellow pink-purple, with ½ inch pinkish-purple, dark purple partially red-purple, a red-purple arm, dark-purple patchy-red pink-purple dark-purple red-purple red-dark purple inch.

What falls out when we shake a tree? Shake the tinticture of scent? Nostrils, amniotic sacs – what bursts?

It goes without saying that the ear is ever open; that little loops in front of mouth are attention encased bubbles; contained in breath like a purpose. Circles without circumferences; cartewheel galaxies. Full blown sun. Gently, we think in such substances, a breath from face to face; sun from peasant to field to bowl to body. Oral curves bear fruit. "Say, don't speak with your mouth full." Costume sun; drench and dry. I've given it up to you. Some hearts tell something good. Some hearts are together against seasons; some hearts are low hung fruit. It's all I've ever wanted. A way to speak precise, quiet and with climate. A way to lounge in sun; flexible radiance, heat that's nothing new to me. It is very bright in the sun. The birds wake us and I am gone from your belly to slowly rise. To set upon some truth in the day as not open, as not a yawning gap, but a mass; the massiveness of our bodies spooning together. Monstrous cuddled forms. Under light, we look silly. My tiny expenditure to your few grams. Under one body, cadence of another body. What a surprise. What unmanageable forms. Say, "the sun hunts us;" all this brightness, getting brighter. This almost very bright in which I'm all that I ever will be. It's all I've ever wanted. To wake up over and over again in this small movement universe. To sun myself. My voice of an angel. Before breakfast and the fall away from warmth.

The sun does not break into pieces. The sun is constant weight. Where am I supposed to be in a landscape under a number of light sources? A perfect body dressing windows. Torso strobe; shit fluorescence (as in something passes through me not my own). Beaten sun; sure particles. Sure, sure oath. As if light, as if delay. Waves of whatever light caught between an infant's prattle and breaking out in a man's cry.

I lost myself a long time ago.

A bowl resting between knees.

Whoops!

It was a matter of time.

Safe as saying "off" again in the dark. Safe as seeing the moon at dawn and knowing that *universe* is catch-all phrase for small moments on your body and also celestial desires.

The mind boggles, doesn't it?

Once I held the shape of heat in my mouth, I found it too much.

Hot lips

wilderness.

Sun that beat our wild-talk.

Once I had the shape of water in my mouth, I found my body.

Goalmouth

lipstick-toyland

the sun that once beat down.

Compressed text; compression locks extravagance: *to not say everything, to say everything at once.*

It was just then our legs and everything, in one fell swoop, dove into fluid inclination. A bowl of milk. A glass of water. Dawn, a spacing; another word for color: carnation. Found alluvial intensity under our lips, in-innards; the sun and our hearts ruling radiance.

I'm wondering, what needs profusion?

If I should say anything at all.

As breath or wind alone fills up holes in bodies.

Wind as another word for "pleasing me."

I'm about it.

Cast fall. Cover up.

Such little ease on the bearing of a curve; bearing of a fruit. Low hanging fruit; then I was the lowest of the low. Testicular with abandon. Testicles in sunset color.

Nothing but whom entanglement.

This palate I am on.

Platelets intake pigeonhole musk.

Arteriovenous laments; subcutaneous teething.

I can unfold my life almost completely.

Show aquifers to your touch and to the heat above.

And to be aghast at the bright.

Cast off; cast bone.

Our bodies in elevation but also the weight of promise.

A body always lets itself be weighed.

Even an eye has mass.

And then, seeing each other's eyes, I groped you like working the land.

Gazed threshed ringlets; glaze thresh minutiae color swallows or spit-ups.

Dawn, a spacing; an instant clarity illuminates us.

For simplicity, say a hand working its offering:

A. Was performing ups and downs for ten to twenty minutes several times over a two to three hour period.

B. Was sweating during and after performing ups and downs, and that the room temperature was probably in the 40-50s degree Fahrenheit range;

C. and seemed to be agitated and continued to talk after doing ups and downs.

It's a matter of letting things go.

Letting it drop.

Flashlights to blossoms.

My empty my stomach all the rage.

Powder anatomy.

Shitting bricks in every direction.

I have a body and this is it.

Feeding time. Feeding light.

Then comes ring-a-round-a-body as if it were the whole world.

Your spiritual receptacle to my treasure trove.

When the small is placed in the large, it fits, yet may still be lost.

Nothing is out of the ordinary.

It becomes brighter.

Mouth bits in empty air.

Then bit by bit, you thrown again to water so that I may have a second chance to save us both. Such little ease of which we have spoken above; namely, that whether we compress little or much, we recoil in equal time. To go one better – I'll say that it's to be careless in language – that I imagine our bodies transparent without any substance passing through them; without light conversation; without dark memories.

Of hoods non-moving. Of all havens gone.

The simpler the image, the vaster the dream.

Of an anywhere that incurs our tiny grams; those tiny grams that open a space: a pasture, a hive or something excavated, even a closure as long there is a tone. A pipsqueak. Yes, one of mouths or corners, but in both, a passage from I to we. Quiet blossom. Quite carnal color. And then we reach, this is the way we are, and the trick is turned. We were the lowest of the low; *this is the way we are* – half arc of daylight, length of daylight – desire diameters; forced drift.

HEXBUGONIA
Nikki Sheppy

druthers guile
stars of pollen
a body hell
she and all
the shes arrive
in atmospheres
of catabolic oil
and heat
dove no quiet
slow slow
slake jelly
to birth the
anabolic dawn

loamed alone
plenum heat
a bull heaven
a bull shanty
routinely meat
bruises cowl
and sphinx a
buttery lumen
abyssal hiss
the bowel hexed
hunting how
regular tilings
of the animal

furs aghast
plummet softly
sphenic or spheric
bone and joint
a sapped halving
awaits a whole
tensile prehensile
precedent of proxies
a feral cadaver
collapsed with
contagion fucked
up all his tender
dying wishes

bloods pupate
haw numina
the gripping droves
data estrous
and boiling mud
even ghosts
burn half-jam they
are liking licking
cells corrode it's
the nymphical now
detonations
mother inside
a noised rot pelt

often hewn
a paucity
of said child
pollen-blooming
rake so full
of blood
the variegations
purging into
acute night
that is
deep difference
mouth of mouth
speaking cult

rilled and buried
flight path
the groping drones
from the pelt
and the queen
exiting
on a wing and a
warm cedar-
scented oxygen
collapsed hollow
the day awol
a windless fur
sun of her

AESTHETICIZE
Nikki Sheppy

inside where only i am i am also impossible for which there can be no cure so now the interiors multiply a *topos* of surgical entries bushwhacking through the inner salt and the carbon thistle of all human belonging our gut opens its duplicity like magnificence in a gun-grey hithering ballroom where the atomic dance is a many-splendoured circling of chance and nuclear attraction we now double or treble the tongue that lamps over what is not happening in the beauty of all these acres that wick to burn and subsume their own tallow the inside leverages pleats and lipids to settle its fields with décor well-appointed yes we speak our lovely

a swell small hunkering beneath loud metal it furnishes me with paralysis as if my stillness could purchase freedom from the fear of making noise cupped thought is the only way to roam here in the wilderness room so let's beautify the darkness peel a dual star system from the mind and sticker it on the wall to bask in luminous exception all pulsed actuality crafts a girly subversion now think about dessert the critical fiction of our sugar both seizure and desertion sweetness cultivated and precluded as when contagions spread treaties and armour the muscle is brash stunning and cruel it is such a friend i liken it to liking our enmity as loveliest war *antigène ce qui réagit dans l'intérieur du soi* for the sake of health *comme la beauté du mutisme qui suis-je? ici encore en corps silencieux tout pèse légèrement irréaliste* a helluva house *je me coince parmi les douces clôtures* of minute sensation *c'est le travail inoubliable et cellulaire* it propels me to the crux dense with logistics *et là je trouve ce nous fétichiste nœud de nos plusieurs intérieurs* as if our selves exceeded the topological possibilities *de cette chambre qui grossit sans règles* and with a mathematical glory not unlike Kantian sublimity of course such things *poussent dans le sol qui sème l'armoire infinitésimale*: iota's resurrected *animal(e)*

assume insignificance *une séquence dans laquelle elle s'abolit* zeroes approach the infinitude in which *le charme d'un chiffre diabolique me séduit* and it is possible even desirable by dint of calculation to locate *le viol qui me touche de façon désarmante* the transcendental uncountable *précision de mon sang de mes poumons de mon numéro immense et secret* cantilevering an algorithm over *l'abîme inarticulé* what was its beauty? to be calculable or to defy all tabulation? or between *là dedans parmi l'enfance et les blessures des petits qui ne comprennent pas encore comment* what counts is always bigger *et qui découvrent la splendeur en tout ce qui est subtil*

RAPT FRACTURES I-IV
Natalie Simpson

I.

An ambulance pitch. Fresh snow. The scene below. Soft leaf peel. Mapped interior, bursting inner mischief. Stems teem to trunks. Vernacular. Strips of treed. A sleeve of hurt stirs. We rain voluminous spurrings.

Thunderous governance. Tamping the russet grid.

We have purpled our being. The sun lingers voluption. Our longing confides in our reticence. Gathering morning. Wrought firmly, it skims the gentle manifest. Spooling loop, a torn blue consequence. Leaf light. A shadow vein.

Coming through thickets, through sadness, plaingrass, ontogeny. Tap actuals. Coming through fervour, reluctance, taming.

II.

Place here fashion and here the assault. Place here derision. Shame and pickled insolence. Trace here succulence, our tender bones. Taste here craven, here malleable. Stem here brutal. Looming, succinct. Ship symmetry. Shape soothing. Here tailing, here tame ambiance. Scale here reverence, institutional, dooming. Tell scrim.

We have whispered slope essentials. Unwieldy spooling pockets of loss. The tense eruption of feeling into plastic, into the ecstatic real.

III.

Picture this then occurring. A strong spill of essence. A calm mask. Torturing home. The blessed fallacies pile. The wanton notions. Recuperate the falling star points, pocks of light in the glossy spill. Suppose a railing outward, a tall long winnowing. Suppose an emotional segregation, stamped-out form. A flame infringing. Suppose a mollusc, hardened shell, grave wood musk. Suppose it crawls. Circling fresh shoots. Tense saturation, verbs quavering on branches, caught rain pooled in them. The gaunt blossoms bend. Terrestrial, and filtered. Suppose it coincides.

IV.

Windows shade implication. We root particulars, we dreg. Take shame to task. Take lustre to shine. Hanging baskets from ledges, wind-blown, arid stunned eruptions.

The frantic correspondence of laundry and order. The pillowing altitudes. Trick this matter, tumble it to symbols, fraught and tender hauntings, the word behind the word behind the casting.

Fumigated storerooms, musk of root vegetables, dust in trailing clumps. Gaze takes its salty fill, about faces, dims. The shrill essentials pool. Parade elation. Scatter burn. Ox turn. The tilling masks a deep division, the soil flasks rain.

REMOVING THE SHOE
Emily Ursuliak

Pedro, corralled,
        lame
   in his hind
      leg,
            he holds them back,

     inflamed
         hoof
              suspended,
    tip
        pressing
            half
        crescents
in sand.

      Art and Martin
         and other
construction camp workers
          gather,
resting arms
        on fence rails.
They offer suggestions.

Silent,
the girls have decided

    to stick to the sidelines,
        pleased
            with the workforce
       they've gathered.

    The solution resolved:
        remove Pedro's shoe.

The men vault the corral,
      edging
           toward Pedro,
                ropes
                ready.

  At Pedro's head,
      Art buckles
  the halter.

Martin cuts
        for the rear,
    rope in hands
        for a sling.

A pop
      of pushed
          air,
    a hoof
        cuts past
            his ear,

        and a deacon,
                running to join
Art at the front,
                    the two of them:

    knuckles
        hook
            throat latch

    fingers
        braid to
            cheek
            plate.

They hold Pedro
            steady,
        their legs spread
ready
        as gunslingers.

Martin,
    side stepping
the posterior,

        the slick
            hiss
of Pedro's tail
        whipping,
            enraged.
A lunge
    for the leg —

       Martin's hand
              clasps it
                     at last.

Pedro rears,
       but careens,
              off-balance
      body
             crashing
                      groundward.

Pedro,
       winded,
cheek
       crushed
             to sand,
forelock
       smeared
              over eye,

              but out snakes
                     his upper lip
             twitching
                  for a blade
                        of grass.
Anne and Phyl
             exhale relief.

        Art
        and the deacon
             pull him back
                   to standing.

    Martin
        loops
   the rope,
      hoof
            in hand now,

   one palm
        on hock,
   other pulling
            pastern,

        collapsing
    the leg in
coiled
spring,
    the sling cinched
    tight,

    all weight
         on cannon bone
    braced
         on knee;
    right hand
        waves

    for nail pullers,
                    passed nimble.

The shoe
      embosses
the sand,

and Pedro
     walks
          free.

STEPHANIE MCMAHON'S PERFECT EYELINER
Natalie Zina Walschots

dagger or heel, your gaze all stiletto
getting colour with a glance
unblemished scalp, no razors hidden in tape
a wicked expanse of fingernail

best for business is
making them juice the hard way
office or abbatoir, every contract
a crimson mask

all your unravelling tape is red
your HR bladejobs off the Muta Scale
severing arteries, mixing with sweat
plucking coins from the scars
in Abdullah the Butcher's forehead

eating scripts, diamond-edged
brand manager in the business of charring flesh
dripping, raw

HEAVY METALS
Natalie Zina Walschots

Metallica – *Master of Puppets*

Some cultures used thorns. Others, needles or silver or bone. The suture could be made of silk, strips of an animal's muscle, tendons, hemp thread. Ants might be coaxed to bite the edges of the wound, and once their mandibles locked, the bodies would be twisted off, leaving a row of jaws and heads holding torn flesh together. Carbolic catgut and chromic catgut. Polyvinyl alcohol. A square knot, a surgeons knot. Blanching of the skin. Simple interrupted stitch.

Iron Maiden – *The Number of the Beast*

Will it come from the sea or from the earth? Blasphemous names carved on seven heads, lion's mouth and leopard's body, crowned and wounded. Or, lamb-horned and dragon-voiced, bearer of an ugly mark. Which beast's boiling scars will we follow?

Slayer – *Reign In Blood*

From gouts to thick ropes, as platelets collide and fibrin knots the clotting. From liquid to lumpy unctuousness, fat globs of tissue, blood becomes organ, becomes body. Slit throat of a pale prince, lips blue, bleeding out.

Pantera – *Vulger Display of Power*

Rubber now, originally shaped from rhinoceros hide. Three to five feet long, a full inch thick at the base, tapering to less than a quarter at the tip. Rolled between heavy plates until it becomes a tapered cylinder. Cattle driving, killing snakes, crowd control, judicial discipline.

Black Sabbath – *Sabbath Bloody Sabbath*

Most were accused of poisoning wells, eating babies, desecrating the host or Eucharist, and kissing Satan's anus.

EVERYTHING ELSE IS SCALE
Andrew Wedderburn

On the Moon the surveyors drive iron stakes into the grey rock according to their map. The surveyors run long silver string-lines between the stakes to mark edges. They fly still steel flags from high poles to mark points.

They leave their tents on the Moon and take long floating steps towards the worksite. Bounding strides that arc across the black Moon sky, loaded down with their burdens: food for the day in galvanized lunchboxes, boots and gloves and goggles, picks and shovels. They bring hammer drills to pierce deep into the Moon on the points marked by the surveyors. Explosives to feed into the drill-holes inserted deeply into the Moonskin. The explosive-carriers lag behind and take carefuller strides, each parabolic step more deliberate at the bottom, loose knees cushioning their burden.

"From here to here," says the foreman, pointing down the line.

They clap gloved hands to the sides of their heads and turn their faces from the noise and shock of each deeply buried explosion. The ground buckles and grey dust billows out from the shaft. Diffuses into the Moon sky, a dense, free smear against the black behind it. The charges break and shatter the rock, free it in tiny pieces to float away from formations hardened into long, long before.

On the Moon they cross gloved hands and lean on shovelshafts to look up into the sky. More stars than they'd ever seen wheel above them. Any constellations they may have known in an old life filled and made different by new stars, hidden previously by the fog of atmosphere. Or maybe, someone thinks, looking into this overgrown sky, they only hadn't looked for so long. There wasn't a lot of time before for looking upwards at night. They look up and the dust of their detonations settles on uplifted faces, finely sifted powder, icing sugar snow on a winter night, somewhere back below them where there are still winters.

UP-BELT
Andrew Wedderburn

On the news she ate raw seal meat and you smelt iron through the vacuum tube.

"We can't call it organic beef anymore on account of the wood preservative in the fence posts it was pull them all out of the ground or lose the certification so just take our word for it that they ate root raw grass off the hardpan and slept outside."

Skimmilk white and home early from work so we gave him cigarettes until he'd composed himself enough for "See when you're working on the deboning line you just zone right out the same motion over and over again Grab Jab Twist Jimmy," and "Sometimes the bone comes right out and sometimes it's like a lock with the tumblers all wore down and you've got to really jimmy that key," and eventually "I've told you that before you just zone out, an arm on a box, the same motion the same motion, left hand grab right hand jab, and then up-belt from me he let go of his knife it rolled in front of me he

Watched her eat raw seal meat with her fingers and went down the block to the Shoppers Drug Mart for a Tetrapack of chicken broth and microwaved a white bowlful.

reached across for it see and like I said you're just zoned out just Grab Jab Twist Jimmy.

FROM SHARE REACT: A MEMOIR IN FOUR CHILDREN'S BOOKS
Julia Williams

"We are the one species on the planet capable of limitless imagination and vision, and how do we use our extraordinary mental gifts? To weave lies, to ignore evidence, to render ourselves willfully blind."
  David Suzuki

Two Babies

This one, I hated. Substitute teachers loved it, so there was a lot of sitting on the carpet while they held it up and read it kind of from the side and behind, the way teachers do.

There were different editions and all of them had awful illustrations. Minnie Mouse eyelashes on the glass baby, fake Japanese woodcut waves, watercolours — cartoonish or faux artsy and nothing in between. I outgrew the story and then I forgot it, and just when I'd forgotten it, it came back, now as required reading for a university literature course. I had to buy it.

It's a critique of colonialism. It's a parable of the immigrant experience. It's a investigation of traditional craftsmanship. The paper baby is Japan or the paper baby is Vietnam or the paper baby is China. The glass baby is Venice or Holland or England. The island (for it was an island) is America. Or it's death. Or enlightenment.

I graduated and dropped the book in a charity bin. Then, earlier this year, I heard a woman reading *Two Babies* on the radio backed by some extremely moody electronica, and a week later I heard it again, and I realized it's not going away, ever.

But I hate it. It's the sort of children's story adults like. They think the story, like the sea, is deep and wide and full of lost souls.

But *Two Babies* is just a love story. That's why it frightens children.

↭

Here's a thing I found about the woman's voice and the moody electronica. Apparently it's a sound painting.

Reprinted with permission from *Fast Forward Weekly*, week of November 9, 2013

Recording Restored
Local musician restores cassette recovered from a demolished Victoria Park home
By Nicole Raven

Local musician Charles Grant is restoring and digitizing a collection of tape reels discovered in a Victoria Park home in 2010. The recordings, believed to have been made by a former resident of the home, were purchased in an estate sale held shortly before the residence was destroyed to make way for Stampede expansion.

"It's just a little shoebox of tape reels. I put it on one side and forgot about it," Grant says. "I never gave it a listen until a few weeks ago. I was blown away." The recordings include handwritten liner notes dated 1990 that identify the creator as "Mary C". A combination of ambient electronic music, children's stories and what appear to be found recordings, the body of work is described by Grant as a "sound painting."

According to Grant, whoever made the recordings appears to have been a promising amateur. "It's rough in spots but there's just something about it. You kind of want to sit down and have a conversation with this person," Grant says. "It's very intimate. It's kind of like she was making a soundtrack for her own life."

A conversation between Grant and Mary C. is unlikely to happen in the near future — the recording artist's current whereabouts is unknown. Grant has been unsuccessful in his attempts to find her. "There's not much to go on."

Meanwhile, Grant is digitizing the tape reels one track at a time and making them available online at maryc.ca. The reels are water-damaged, and Grant says he's determined to get the best sound quality possible. "I'm not superstitious, but I feel like it came my way for a reason. The box just sat in that house all that time. There must have been so many renters through there and nobody ever picked it up."

SUNSET GROCERY
Rita Wong

at eight years old the cash register's metallic rhythm comes quick to my fingers: 59¢ from $1.00 gets you back one penny, one nickel, one dime, one quarter. could do this backwards in my sleep, & probably have, but i prefer stocking shelves. prefer to avoid customers making snotty fake chinese accents, avoid men flipping through porn. open nine to nine seven days a week, the store is where i develop the expected math skills: $60 net one day divided by twelve hours is $5 an hour, divided by two people is $2.50 an hour, or divided by five people $1.00 an hour.

occupied with small details, sunset grocery can be duller than counting the 20,000 times i breathe each day. i sell cigarettes i am not allowed to smoke: player's light, export a, du maurier. nicotine variations, drum & old port. popsicles, twinkies, two percent milk. 7-up, coffee crisp, bottles of coke. faced with these cancer- & cavity-inducing goods, i retreat into books. by grade four i learn the word "inscrutable," & practice being so behind the cash register. however, i soon realize that i am read as inscrutable by many customers with absolutely no effort on my part, so i don't bother trying any more. ten years of this means you can one day leave when someone takes your place. what changes?

a skinny hallway connects three bedrooms in the back. i share a room with my sister. our dog Smoky often sleeps by the bunk bed. she snores. my sister talks in her sleep. down the hall my father snores too. some nights, it's hard to tell who snores louder—the dog or my dad. the nights are noisy with all the things never said in the day.

the summer that i am afraid of fire, i hold Smoky every night until the fear subsides. until my heart slows enough that i can sleep. her stinky breath comforts me, reminds me of the many senses we have to discover fire before it finds us.

the summer that i am afraid of fire, i always have a glass of water near my bed. not enough to put out flames, i can at least drink when i awaken, throat dry, sweaty & fearful in the night.

maybe because i am a fire girl, sparked between my parents' loins in more romantic times, i know the power of fire, how it creates heat in cold prairie winters, how it simmers, boils & stirfries countless meals in the steaming kitchen, how it rests hungry within me, waiting for the tinder of another body. the fear stems from fire's power to destroy, to erase an existence eked out from penny nickel dime tedium. to consume in minutes what took years to build.

one ear always attuned to the bell of the opening door i find i can't trust or tell a straight story. what if flamboyant prometheus had been an archer shooting down suns instead of bearing fire into human hands? i draw witches with pointy hats & greenblack hair, dragon ladies in salem garb, learn of ancient chinese secrets from american laundry soap commercials. between amazons, milwaukee factory girls, flying nuns, customers come in, customers go out. rabbits, cheese, women populate the moon. flame throwers light the sky with their arms' circular logic.

part fire, part water, part air & part earth, i try to distance myself
from the fire within, fear that i cannot control its random blasts.
i learn to cultivate that part of me which is earth, sowing gradual
seeds of pragmatism, small quiet sprouts in the spring, studious
endeavours reaping scholarly harvests, parental approval,
respectable tunnels for escape.

as months grow into years, the fears go undercover, as do the
dreams. the connection between night & day is too painful
& so each morning i cross the river of waking washed clean of
nocturnal memory. the price for a respectable daytime existence
is high. it is my own desire. creating a vacuum,
the hollow space which i become.

when i return to the grocery store years later, that long echoing
childhood hallway seems dark, crowded, needing new carpet,
clean linoleum, anything to open it up, clear it of
so many night words still unheard.

GRAMMAR POEM
Rita Wong

write around the absence, she said, show
its existence
demonstrate   *this is*
its contours   *the sound of*
how it   *my chinese tongue*
tastes   *whispering*: nei tou
where   gnaw ma? *no*
its edges   *tones can*
fall   *survive this*
hard   *alphabet*
on my stuttering tongue, how its tones &
              pictograms get flattened out by the
                    steamroller of the english language,
live   its etymology of
half-submerged   assimilation
in the salty home of   tramples budding
my mother tongue,   memory into sawdusty
shallows   stereotypes, regimented capitals,
                        arrogant nouns & more nouns,
                   punctuated by subservient descriptors.
grammar is the dust on the streets waiting to be washed off by immigrant
cleaners or blown into your eyes by the wind. grammar is the invisible
net in the air, holding your words in place. grammar, like wealth,
belongs in the hands of the people who produce it.

GALLUS
Eric Zboya

SOLARIUM 1
Eric Zboya

THE DESTRUCTIVE IMPULSE BECOMES AUTOMATIC
Paul Zits

The destructive impulse becomes automatic
    Sergio González Rodríguez, from *The Femicide Machine*

•

The place was aglow with red and blue lights, with the naked body arched across the old mattress. Face up and dead, she was naked except for an unlaced pair of worn-out blue-green high-top sneakers. Her body was sprawled sideways across an old mattress from which her head dangled into the bottles and leaves. Red and blue lights upon her while she slumbered. Red and blue lights upon her as if she speaks. Like a gas flame, upon her throat, a four-pointed star. Like a cardinal's robe, upon her head. Like a garland of lupins, upon her arm. Red and blue lights upon her while she slumbered. Like a tomato, upon her breast. Like a marble, upon her shoulder. Like a cockatoo's bared crown, upon her rug of fur and her little eyes. Like the turquoise stone in the belly of the Thunderbird, upon her limbs. Red and blue lights upon the soil, nearby. Like the lining of a crucible upon her neck. Red and blue lights upon her exposed years. Upon her life. Upon her death. Like cold glass upon her heels. Like the worms on which small fish feed upon her breast. Red and blue lights upon her light freckles and short red hair. Like the flames on a gas range upon her head. Full upon her face, a tangled mass. Like a piece of iron cooling in the air, slashing now, upon her face, her head, her chest and her abdomen, clear down, even to her hands and feet. Red and blue lights upon her hands, indeed as if sleeping. Like jam upon her knee. Like skin that had been badly bruised upon her lips. Like brick upon the plane of her body. Upon her fragile form. Like the touch paper you light, swooping down upon her and then circling like a great gull in the wind. Like the 20-note lira upon her finger. Like fingernails upon her shoulders. Upon her open palm. Upon her shoulders. Sweeping down upon her shoulders. Like tinsel caught in the breeze upon her canals. Upon her knees. Like a live coal upon her lips. Like a slab of sky off the assembly line upon her face. Like a depot stove in midwinter in her cradle. Like faded grass upon her loveliness and perfection in that setting. Upon her body. Like arterial blood upon her shores. Red and blue light along her small tin pail, nearby. Along her large tin pail, nearby. Like the beryls in the clasp of the Queen's missal along her sides. Like Japanese lacquer along her back. Red and blue lights along her notebook, nearby. Like kingfisher feathers along her side. Along her towering side. Like rubies along her sides. Along her entire body. Like the Sycorax's eyes along her sides. Like a turkey cock along her jawline. Like a ribbon along her side. Like raspberries along her spine. Like the shadow of a woman's eyes along her spine. Like the hands of a woman scrubbing along her throat. Like delphiniums and bachelor buttons along her spine. Like flashing lightening along her jawline and hooked under her ears. Like radishes along her upper-gums. Like the color given off by burning chemicals along her stomach. Like a cock's comb along her cheekbones. Like neon woven into cloth along her jaw line. Like a girl's nipples in love along her freckles. Like roads along her neck. Like crayfish along her upper-teeth. Like a sulphur flame along her sides. Like cinnabar along her forearm. Like chalk along her leg. Red and blue lights along her jacket, nearby. Like sundae cherries along her shoulder. Like skimmed-milk along her sides. Like the Little Red Spot of Jupiter along her neck. Like the sky after a storm along her shoulder and side. Along her side. Like cobalt glass along her sides. Like a crab along her supine frame. Along her spine. Along her spine. Along her spine. Like rotten meat along her cheeks. Along her cheekbones. Like embers along her temple. Like the back wall of a rat's cage along her waist. Along her waist. Like smoke from a burning building along her body. Like a peacock's neck along her spine. Like the blood of a slaughtered ox along her length. Like a bruise along her eyes, opened then closed. Like some crafty old monkey along her back. Like faded denim along her arm, leg, belly. Like wattles against her abdomen. Like a fig against her head. Like the dawning stain from the East against her bare skin. Like young wheat against her ribs. Like a wound against her cheek. Like dark byssus against her chest. Like pomegranate seeds against her body. Like rippling silk against her shoulder. Like the buffalo skull against her face. Like shadowed waters against her throat. Like surgery against her mouth. Like the inside of a saxophone against her wrist. Like a sausage against her ear. Like a wagon track against her side. Like the stripes in the U.S. flag against her throat. Against her throat. Like a bit of old Delft against her thighs. Like ledger lines against her caved-in-chest. Like stars made of thread on the pillowcase against her breastbone. Red and blue lights against her earrings. Like a cactus blossom against her face. Like a fine pale porcelain against her bare belly. Like corral against her skull. Like the shadow of Glaucus against her breast. Like a scalped head against her long long legs.

THE STIRRING OF THE SLATED METAL BLINDS
Paul Zits

•

The stirring of the slated metal blinds. A breeze unsteadies the bottom rail. A cadence clatters identical with that playing back through the speakers. Greater breezes asphyxiate on the slats. Identical with the playback. The calculating machines ticking away upstairs. Identical. Breezes and greater breezes enter through a gap between the lower sash and the sill. The valence, yellowed and damp, lies at the base of the wall, beneath the window. The window is an interior casing, a head jamb, a side jamb, an upper sash, a sash lock, a lower sash, a top rail, a bottom rail, a stile, a muntin, an exterior sill, a stool, an apron and panes. The window is six panes in the upper sash and six panes in the lower. Sliding the blinds to the side, exposing the bottom left-hand pane, notice a square of sulphured newsprint pasted to fit precisely with its frame. The fitting of the newsprint has clipped the image of a Zeppelin in half. The engines, rudder and elevator-flap with a blue sky the backdrop. The sun has washed the page of its material. It is pale. The ink is deserting the page. The image is unknotted, nearly vapour. Transparent in the light, muddied with lettering from the backside. The Zeppelin is the bottom left pane of the lower sash. The picture of a painting of Wernher von Braun's wheel-shaped space station design is the bottom middle pane of the lower sash. A pudgy Shakur, thug-life tattooed across his belly is the bottom right pane of the lower sash. An image of a painting of a pipe is the top right pane of the lower sash. A reproduction of a painting of Aphrodite, flanked by slave-boys, each made to resemble Eros, who cool her with their fans, is the top middle pane of the lower sash. Zindapir, royally clad in blue and crimson Mughal dress, a green turban on his head, riding along the Indus on a palla fish is the top left pane of the lower sash. The upper sash is revealed by pulling the cord tassel. Lenin is the bottom left pane of the upper sash, seated at the Cafe Rotonde on a cane chair; he has paid twenty centimes for his coffee, with a tip of one sou. He is drinking out of a small white porcelain cup. He is wearing a bowler hat and a smooth white collar…He is teaching himself to govern one hundred million people. A photograph of a painting of the Last Supper on a grain of rice is the bottom middle pane of the upper sash. Saturn devouring his sons is the bottom right pane of the upper sash. Adolph Hitler is the top right pane of the upper sash. A reproduction of a painting of dead fish and oysters on a kitchen slab, dominated by the rearing, arched shape of a gutted snake is the top middle pane of the upper sash. A scenery with a small house in the top left corner is the top right pane of the upper sash. Light comes in in its pieces, its colors with threads, through the reclining nude, through the arousal, the panicking, the succession of landscapes, the palpable lifelikeness, the skies, the heat and thirst, the ugly blue and orange of the optimum fire. From the doorway looking back, through a door that is always open, or nearly always, a Coninxloo-like scenery, or the sky of a planetarium, washes over the room, the stirring of the slated metal blinds.

CONTRIBUTORS

Hollie Adams is originally from Windsor, Ontario. She has an MA in English and Creative Writing from the University of Windsor and a PhD in English from the University of Calgary. She currently lives part-time in Calgary and part-time in Red Deer, where she teaches English at Red Deer College. Her writing has been published in several magazines across Canada, including *Prairie Fire, The Antigonish Review*, and *Carousel*, as well as on *McSweeney's Internet Tendency* and in an anthology of short fiction inspired by the band Broken Social Scene. Her first novel, a second-person comedy about grief called *Things You've Inherited From Your Mother*, was published in 2015 by NeWest Press.

Jonathan Ball holds a PhD in English and teaches literature, film, and writing at the University of Manitoba and the University of Winnipeg. He is the author of *Ex Machina*, a poetry book about how machines have changed what it means to be human, *Clockfire*, a collection of 77 plays that would be impossible to produce, and *The Politics of Knives*, poems about violence, narrative, and spectatorship, and winner of a Manitoba Book Award. Jonathan also published *John Paizs's Crime Wave*, an academic study of a neglected Canadian cult film classic, which was launched at the Toronto International Film Festival and also won a Manitoba Book Award. He co-edited, with Ryan Fitzpatrick, *Why Poetry Sucks: An Anthology of Humorous Experimental Canadian Poetry*. Jonathan has also directed short films (including *Spoony B*, which sold to The Comedy Network), been a section editor for *The Manitoban* and *filling Station magazine*, served as the managing editor of *dANDelion magazine*, and founded the literary journal *Maelstrom*.

Braydon Beaulieu is a doctoral candidate at the University of Calgary, where he studies creative writing, poetics, science fiction, and digital games. His most recent chapbook, *Thin and Pure*, is available from Chromium Dioxide Press as part of the special edition of Christian Bök's *The Xenotext (Book 1)*. You can find him on Twitter at @braydonbeaulieu.

Derek Beaulieu is the author of the collections of poetry *with wax, fractal economies, chains, silence, ascender / descender, kern, frogments from the frag pool* (co-written with Gary Barwin) and *Please no more poetry: the poetry of derek beaulieu* (Ed. Kit Dobson). He has also written 4 collections of conceptual fiction: *a a novel, flatland, Local Colour* and *How To Write* (Nominated for the W.O. Mitchell Award). He is the author of two collections of essays: *Seen of the Crime* and *The Unbearable Contact with Poets*. Beaulieu co-edited bill bissett's *RUSH: what fuckan theory* (with Gregory Betts) and *Writing Surfaces: fiction of John Riddell* (with Lori Emerson). He is the publisher of the acclaimed no press and is the visual poetry editor at UBUWeb. Beaulieu has exhibited his work across Canada, the United States and Europe and is an award-winning instructor. Derek Beaulieu was the 2014–2016 Poet Laureate of Calgary, Canada.

Christian Bök is the author of *Crystallography* (Coach House Press 1994), a pataphysical encyclopedia nominated for the Gerald Lampert Memorial Award, and of *Eunoia* (Coach House Books 2001), a bestselling work of experimental literature, which has gone on to win the Griffin Prize for Poetic Excellence. Bök has created artificial languages for two television shows: Gene Roddenberry's *Earth: Final Conflict* and Peter Benchley's *Amazon*. Bök has also earned many accolades for his virtuoso performances of sound poetry (particularly the *Ursonate* by Kurt Schwitters). His conceptual artworks (which include books built out of Rubik's cubes and Lego bricks) have appeared at the Marianne Boesky Gallery in New York City as part of the exhibit *Poetry Plastique*. Bök is currently a Professor of English at Charles Darwin University. His most recent book is *The Xenotext (Book 1)* (Coach House Books 2015).

Louis Cabri's stuff includes *Posh Lust* (New Star Books), *Poetryworld* (Capilano University Editions), *The Mood Embosser* (Coach House Books), and thingies like *Poems* (Olive), *What Is Venice?* (Wrinkle), — *that can't* (Nomados), and *Curdles* (housepress). Curated projects he's done include the poets' talk series *Projector Verse* (with Listen Chen and Cecily Nicholson) for the Kootenay School of Writing, the poets' exchange *PhillyTalks* (with Aaron Levy), a sound and poetry issue for *ESC: English Studies in Canada* (with Peter Quartermain), open letters to/from poets for *Open Letter* (with Nicole Markotić), and *hole magazine* and books (with Rob Manery). He's written on poetry of Catriona Strang, Lissa Wolsak, Jackson Mac Low, Roy Miki, Bruce Andrews, Fred Wah, among others, and teaches modern and contemporary poetry and poetics, literary theory, and creative writing at the University of Windsor.

Natalee Caple is the author of seven books of poetry and fiction and the co-editor of an anthology of contemporary Canadian writers. The *New York Times* called her fiction "moving … unsettling." The *Washington Post* described her writing as "breathlessly good." Caple's latest novel, *In Calamity's Wake*, was published by HarperCollins in Canada and by Bloomsbury in the US. She is a professor of English, teaching Canadian literature and Creative Writing at Brock University.

Weyman Chan's second book, *Noise From the Laundry,* was a finalist for the 2008 Governor General's Award for poetry and the Acorn-Plantos People's Poetry Award. His fifth book of poetry, *Human Tissue—a primer for Not Knowing* was published in 2016 by Talonbooks.

Jason Christie's poetry has appeared in numerous journals and magazines. He is the author of *Canada Post* (Snare), *i ROBOT* (Edge/Tesseract), *Unknown Actor* (Insomniac), and a co-editor of *Shift & Switch: New Canadian Poetry* (Mercury). Two of his chapbooks were nominated for the bpNichol Chapbook Award: *GOVERNMENT* (above/ground), and *Cursed Objects* (above/ground). His most recent chapbook is called *The Charm* (above/ground). He is a past poetry collective member of *filling Station magazine*, *dANDelion magazine*, and currently reviews poetry for *Arc magazine*. He organized and hosted the YARD reading series in Calgary, which took place in his backyard and in the Auburn Saloon.

Chris Ewart recently earned his doctorate with distinction in English & Disability Studies at Simon Fraser University. His novel, *Miss Lamp* (Coach House Books 2006), was shortlisted for a 2007 ReLit Award. His critical work appears in the *Journal of Literary and Cultural Disability Studies*, *Shift: A Journal of Visual and Material Culture*, *Poetic Front*, the book *Global Rights and Perceptions*, a chapter on Samuel Beckett in *Disability, Avoidance and the Academy: Challenging Resistance* (Routledge 2015) and a forthcoming chapter about heroines and the prosthetic in popular culture in *The Matter of Disability* (U Michigan 2017). His short fiction appears in *West Coast Line* and poetry in *Open Letter*, *Canadian Literature* and *Why Poetry Sucks: An Anthology of Humorous Experimental Canadian Poetry* (Insomniac 2014). In addition to teaching Creative Writing and English at SFU, he has taught at University of Calgary, Alberta College of Art and Design, Fairleigh Dickinson University, Vancouver, and was an arts writer for the *Calgary Herald*. He now teaches at Emily Carr University of Art + Design. His work often explores disability and normalcy in literature, film, popular culture and art.

Aaron Giovannone's books of poetry are *The Loneliness Machine* (Insomniac 2014) and *The Nonnets* (Book Thug forthcoming 2018). He has a Ph.D. from the University of Calgary, and he has taught literature and writing at Brock University, l'Università degli Studi di Siena, and Okanagan College.

Helen Hajnoczky is the author of *Poets and Killers: A Life in Advertising* (Snare/Invisible Publishing 2010) and *Magyarázni* (Coach House Books 2016). Helen's chapbook *Bloom and Martyr* won the Kalamalka Press' 2015 John Lent Poetry Prose Award. The poem "Other Observations" has previously appeared in a chapbook of the same name (No Press 2010) and on the *Dusie* blog as "Tuesday Poem #109" (2015). Her poetry has also appeared in the anthologies *Why Poetry Sucks* (Insomniac Press 2014) and *Ground Rules* (Chaudiere Books 2013), as well as in a variety of magazines and chapbooks.

Mason Hastie mostly works in design but also toils secretly in audio. He graduated from ACAD around the turn of the century. He likes brushed metal, and the sweet smell of old circuit boards.

Susan Holbrook's poetry books are the Trillium-nominated *Joy Is So Exhausting* (Coach House Books 2009), *Good Egg Bad Seed* (Nomados 2004) and *misled* (Red Deer 1999), which was shortlisted for the Pat Lowther Memorial Award and the Stephan G. Stephansson Award. *Throaty Wipes* was published by Coach House in 2016. She teaches North American literatures and Creative Writing at the University of Windsor. She recently published a textbook entitled *How to Read (and Write About) Poetry* (Broadview 2015) and is the co-editor of *The Letters of Gertrude Stein and Virgil Thomson: Composition as Conversation* (Oxford 2010). From 1991–1997 she lived in Calgary, where she learned that poetry was not just for extolling Nature but also where Van Gogh's palette in golden foothills against navy sky was so damn poetic!

Ken Hunt's work has appeared in small press editions from Chromium Dioxide, No Press and Spacecraft Press and in *Rampike*, *NōD*, and *Matrix* magazines. His first book of poetry, *Space Administration*, was published in 2014 by the LUMA Foundation as part of Hans Ulrich and Kenneth Goldsmith's *89+ Project*. For three years, Ken served as managing editor of *NōD Magazine,* and for one year, he served as poetry editor of *filling Station.* In 2014, Ken founded Spacecraft Press, a publisher of experimental writing inspired by science and technology. Ken is currently pursuing an English MA at Concordia University in Montréal.

Jani Krulc's first collection of short fiction, *The Jesus Year,* was published in 2013 by Insomniac Press. Jani has an MA in English and Creative Writing from Concordia University, and a BA (Hons) in English from the University of Calgary. She lives and writes in Calgary, where she also teaches and practices Yoga.

Larissa Lai is a novelist, poet and critic, based at the University of Calgary, where she holds a Canada Research Chair in Creative Writing in the English Department. She is the author of six books, including a critical monograph, *Slanting I, Imagining We: Asian Canadian Literary Production in the 1980s and 1990s,* and the novel *Salt Fish Girl*. A recipient of the Astraea Foundation Emerging Writers' Award, she has been shortlisted for the Books in Canada First Novel Award, the Tiptree Award, the Sunburst Award, the City of Calgary W.O. Mitchell Award, the bpNichol Chapbook Award, the Dorothy Livesay Prize and the Gabrielle Roy Prize for Criticism. Her work has been widely performed, studied and reviewed in Europe, Asia, North America and Australia.

Natalie Lauchlan is a Calgary-based emerging performance and installation artist. After receiving her BFA in Craft + Emerging Media from the Alberta College of Art + Design, Natalie began a residency-based practice travelling and working in several countries and a variety of programs as she explores the language of time and memory through the visual language of objects, place, poetry and movement.

Born in England, **Naomi K. Lewis** grew up in Washington, DC and Ottawa, and has since lived in Toronto, Fredericton, Edmonton, and Calgary. She wrote the 2008 novel *Cricket in a Fist* and the 2012 story collection *I Know Who You Remind Me Of*, which was shortlisted for the George Bugnet Award for fiction and the Alberta Readers Choice Award, and won Enfield & Wizenty's Colophon Prize. With Rona Altrows, she co-edited the award-winning 2013 anthology *Shy*. In Edmonton and Calgary, she worked as a magazine editor for ten years, and her magazine journalism has been shortlisted for provincial and national magazine awards. Naomi teaches creative writing, and served as the Calgary Public Library's writer in residence in 2011. In 2016, she was writer in residence at the University of New Brunswick but has since returned to Calgary.

Nathaniel Mah is an emerging Calgary-based photographer. His photography practice deals primarily with solitude, isolation, and the freedom associated with being alone. These themes developed from the solitary time he has spent exploring Calgary and surrounding area. As a high-performance Nordic Combined Athlete, Nathaniel knows the back-country well, and after a serious head-injury in 2014, photography became his focus as he was forced to take a break from training and competition. Nathaniel continues to pursue his career as an elite athlete and emerging photographer as he tours the world in competition.

Nicole Markotić is a novelist, critic, and poet. Her most recent poetry books include *Whelmed* (Coach House Books) and *Bent at the Spine* (BookThug), and her most recent novel is *Rough Patch* (Arsenal Pulp Press). She has edited a collection of poetry by Dennis Cooley, *By Word of Mouth* (Wilfrid Laurier), written a critical book on disability and literature, *Disability in Film and Literature* (McFarland & Co), and completed an edited collection of essays on Robert Kroetsch (Guernica). She has published in literary journals in Canada, the USA, Australia, and Europe. She edits the chapbook series, Wrinkle Press (publishing such authors as Nikki Reimer, Robert Kroetsch, and Fred Wah), and has worked as a freelance editor, as poetry editor for Red Deer Press, and as fiction editor for NeWest Press. Currently, Nicole Markotić is Professor of Literature, Creative Writing, Disability Studies, and Children's Literature at the University of Windsor.

Suzette Mayr is the author of four novels. Her most recent novel, *Monoceros*, won the ReLit Award, the City of Calgary W.O. Mitchell Book Prize, was longlisted for the 2011 Giller Prize, and shortlisted for a Ferro-Grumley Award for LGBT Fiction, and the Georges Bugnet Award for Fiction. *Monoceros* was also included on *The Globe and Mail*'s 100 Best Books of 2011. Her other novels have been nominated for the regional Commonwealth Writers' Prize, the ReLit Award, and the Henry Kreisel Award for Best First Book. She has done interdisciplinary work with Calgary theatre company Theatre Junction, visual artists Lisa Brawn and Geoff Hunter, and she was a writer-in-residence at the University of Calgary and at Widener University, Pennsylvania. She is a former President of the Writers' Guild of Alberta and teaches Creative Writing at the University of Calgary.

rob mclennan currently lives in Ottawa, where he is home full-time with the two wee girls he shares with Christine McNair. The author of more than thirty books, he won the John Newlove Poetry Award in 2010, the Council for the Arts in Ottawa Mid-Career Award in 2014, and was longlisted for the CBC Poetry Prize in 2012. In March 2016, he was inducted into the VERSe Ottawa Hall of Honour. His most recent titles include *The Uncertainty Principle: stories*, (Chaudiere Books 2014) and the poetry collection *A perimeter* (New Star Books 2016). An editor and publisher, he runs above/ground press, Chaudiere Books (with Christine McNair), *The Garneau Review* (ottawater.com/garneaureview), *seventeen seconds: a journal of poetry and poetics* (ottawater.com/seventeenseconds), *Touch the Donkey* (touchthedonkey.blogspot.com) and the Ottawa poetry pdf annual *ottawater* (ottawater.com). In fall 2015, he was named Interviews Editor at *Queen Mob's Teahouse*, and recently became a regular contributor to both the *Drunken Boat* and *Ploughshares* blogs. He spent the 2007-8 academic year in Edmonton as writer-in-residence at the University of Alberta, and regularly posts reviews, essays, interviews and other notices at robmclennan.blogspot.com

kevin mcpherson eckhoff loves poetry parties and saying "Me me me, me memememe ... mmmmm." *Forge* and *rhapsodomancy* are his fault, as are the final issues of *dANDelion magazine* and *Open Letter*, guest edited with his bff, Jake "The" Kennedy. Sorry! BookThug published *Merz Structure No. 2 Burnt by Children at Play*. Check it! Out! Library-style! When kevin's not teaching at Okanagan College, he hangs out with a Laurel and two kiddos, sometimes cuddling at the Starlight Drive-in during a full moon in July or dipping into Halfway Hotsprings during a light February snowfall. Oh, and you can catch his face as "Tall Security Guard" in the film *Tomato Red*.

Sandy Pool is the author of two full-length poetry collections and one chapbook published by Vallum editions. Her first collection, *Exploding Into Night* (Guernica Editions) was nominated for The Governor General's Award for Poetry. Her second collection, *Undark: An Oratorio* (Nightwood Editions) was nominated for both Ontario's Trillium Book Award for Poetry, and an Alberta Book Award. Sandy also writes for the stage. Her most recent operas were performed by Tapestry New Opera Works, and featured on CBC Radio. Sandy holds both an MFA from the University of Guelph, and a PhD in Poetics and Creative Writing from the University of Calgary.

Sharanpal Ruprai is an Assistant Professor at the University of Winnipeg in the Women's and Gender Studies Department. Her debut poetry collection, *Seva*, was shortlisted for the Stephan G. Stephansson Award for Poetry by the Alberta Literary Awards in 2015.

Ian Sampson is a graduate of the University of Calgary, where he studied creative writing and medieval literature. He has translated poetry from German, French, Italian, and Old English, among other languages, and is currently at work on a version of *Beowulf*. His writing has received several awards, including the Boccaccio Afterlife Award for his adaptation of a novella from the *Decameron* (republished here), the Sir James Lougheed Award of Distinction, the Kathleen and Russell Lane Canadian Writing Award, and a Doctoral Fellowship from the Social Sciences and Humanities Research Council of Canada. He has been an editor at *filling Station Magazine*, a co-host of the Flywheel Reading Series, and a featured performer at the Calgary Blowout. Now living in Providence (where he recently produced visual work for an exhibit on H. P. Lovecraft), he is completing his PhD in English at Brown University.

Jordan Scott is the author of three books of poetry.

Nikki Sheppy is a poet, editor and arts journalist. She has a doctorate in English literature from the University of Calgary. Her book reviews have appeared in *Uppercase Magazine, Alberta Views*, and *Lemon Hound*, and her poetry in *Event, Matrix, Jacket2, Dusie* and *Touch the Donkey*. She serves as Managing Editor of *filling Station Magazine*, Calgary's experimental literary and arts magazine, and a Director of the Board of Alberta Magazine Publishers Association. Sheppy's *Grrrlhood: a ludic suite* won the 2013 John Lent Poetry-Prose Award and was published as a letter-pressed chapbook (Kalamalka 2014).

Natalie Simpson is the author of *accrete or crumble* (LINEbooks 2006) and *Thrum* (Talonbooks 2014). Her poetry has appeared in the anthologies, *Shift & Switch: New Canadian Poetry* (Mercury Press 2005), *Post-Prairie: an Anthology of New Poetry* (Talonbooks 2005), *Shy: an Anthology* (U of A Press, 2013), *Ground Rules: the best of the second decade of above/ground press 2003-2013* (Chaudiere 2013), and *The Best Canadian Poetry in English* 2013 (Tightrope Books). "Surge", a poetry suite from her latest book, *Thrum*, was shortlisted for the John Lent Poetry/ Prose Award in 2013. She studied English literature at the University of Calgary, completing a Master's thesis on Gertrude Stein's sentences, and law at the University of British Columbia. She practices pro bono law in Calgary, Alberta and curates *filling Station Magazine*'s flywheel Reading Series.

Emily Ursuliak writes both fiction and poetry and has an MA in English, with a focus in creative writing, from the University of Calgary. She is the host and producer of CJSW's literary radio show, *Writer's Block*, and teaches creative writing courses for the Alexandra Writers' Centre and other community organizations.

Natalie Zina Walschots is a freelance writer based in Toronto, Ontario. She is the author of *DOOM: Love Poems For Supervillains* (Insomniac 2012) and *Thumbscrews* (Snare 2007), which won the Robert Kroetsch Award for Innovative Poetry. She writes about comic books, video games, combat sports, RPGs, fan fiction, sadomasochism, feminism, CanLit and difficult music. She is currently working on a novel about a henchwoman, a collection of polyamorous fairytales, and exploring the poetic potential of the notes engine in the videogame *Bloodborne*.

Andrew Wedderburn attended the Alberta College of Art and the University of Calgary between 1995 and 2001, dropping out of the former and graduating from the latter after studying creative writing. His stories have been published by *filling Station* and *Alberta Views* magazines. His debut novel, *The Milk Chicken Bomb*, was published by Coach House Books in 2007. In 2008 it was a finalist for the Amazon / Books in Canada First Novel Award, and long-listed for International IMPAC Dublin Literary Award. As a musician (guitar, shouting) Wedderburn has written, recorded and toured extensively as a member of the groups Hot Little Rocket and Night Committee, releasing 7 full-length albums over the last two decades. After 20 years living in Calgary, Wedderburn recently moved back to the farm north of Okotoks, Alberta, where he grew up. He now spends most of his time stuck in traffic on McLeod Trail.

Julia Williams is a writer whose work has appeared in several Canadian literary magazines and the anthology *Shift & Switch: New Canadian Poetry*. A long time ago she wrote a book called *The Sink House*, which was published by Coach House Books. The piece that appears in this anthology is an excerpt from her first nonfiction manuscript, *A Memoir in Four Children's Stories*, which is an exploration of memory, identity and media. Except that it is not really nonfiction, but a series of lies. You should not believe what she tells you.

Rita Wong has written four books of poetry: *undercurrent* (Nightwood 2015), *sybil unrest* (co-written with Larissa Lai, Line Books, 2008) *forage* (Nightwood 2007) and *monkeypuzzle* (Press Gang 1998). *forage* won Canada Reads Poetry 2011. Wong received the Asian Canadian Writers Workshop Emerging Writer Award in 1997, and the Dorothy Livesay Poetry Prize in 2008. With Cindy Mochizuki, she has also authored a collection of graphic essays entitled *perpetual* (Nightwood 2015). Born in the territories of the Tsuu T'ina, Siksika and Stoney First Nations, also known as Calgary, she now lives on the unceded Coast Salish territories known as Vancouver. Learning from and with water, she investigates the relationships between contemporary poetics, social justice, ecology, and decolonization.

Eric Zboya is an experimental poet and visual artist who lives in Calgary's bedroom community of Cochrane, AB. Zboya's work has been published and exhibited in a wide variety of chapbooks, literary journals, magazines, anthologies, art galleries, and museums throughout North America and Europe. He was a finalist for both the 2013 Robert Kroetsch Award for Innovative Poetry and the 2013 Alberta Magazines Showcase Awards selection of poetry.

Paul Zits received his MA in English from the University of Calgary in 2010. *Massacre Street* (UAP 2013), the product of his creative dissertation, went on to win the 2014 Stephan G. Stephansson Award for Poetry. In addition to serving two terms as Writer-in-the-Schools at Queen Elizabeth High School in Calgary, teaching creative writing to students in the Gifted and Talented Education (GATE) program, Zits is a regular instructor with the WGA's WordsWorth Camp at Kamp Kiwanis. Zits is currently an instructor with the Edmonton Poetry Festival's Verse Project.

COLOPHON

Book design by Christine McNair. Typeset in Minion and Quadraat Sans by Christine McNair and Cameron Anstee using Adobe InDesign. Minion is a serif typeface designed by Robert Slimbach and inspired by late Renaissance-era type. The name comes from the traditional naming system for type sizes, in which minion is between nonpareil and brevier, equivalent to modern 7PT type. Slimbach described the design as having "a simplified structure and moderate proportions." Quadraat Sans was designed by Fred Smeijers as a companion to his Quadraat Serif. It is a deeply humanist sans serif that is lively on the page.

The cover image is by Natalie Lauchlan and Nathaniel Mah as part of the *Become Akin* project. *Become Akin* is a performance series made during a residency in downtown Calgary with the Ledge Gallery at ArtsCommons. The performance explores the relationship Calgarians have with their city, and the outsider-insider feeling of a disassociated commuter population. Belonging neither to the street people, the business people, or the downtown-living population, Natalie Lauchlan forcibly belongs by becoming part of the landscape, wedging herself into the physical city to become akin with some part of the community of Calgary.

WWW.CHAUDIEREBOOKS.COM

Library and Archives Canada Cataloguing in Publication

The Calgary renaissance / edited by Derek Beaulieu and Rob McLennan.

isbn 978-1-928107-07-1 (paperback)

1. Canadian literature (English)--Alberta--Calgary. 2. Canadian literature (English)--21st century. I. McLennan, Rob, 1970-, editor II. Beaulieu, D. A. (Derek Alexander), 1973-, editor

ps8257.c3c35 2016   c810.8'09712338   c2016-905943-x